JOY COMPASS

Journey into wellness

Jayme Bushmiaer-Davis

BALBOA.PRESS
A DIVISION OF HAY HOUSE

Balboa Press books may be ordered through booksellers or by contacting:

Balboa Press
A Division of Hay House
1663 Liberty Drive
Bloomington, IN 47403
www.balboapress.com
844-682-1282

Because of the dynamic nature of the Internet, any web addresses or links contained in this book may have changed since publication and may no longer be valid. The views expressed in this work are solely those of the author and do not necessarily reflect the views of the publisher, and the publisher hereby disclaims any responsibility for them.

The author of this book does not dispense medical advice or prescribe the use of any technique as a form of treatment for physical, emotional, or medical problems without the advice of a physician, either directly or indirectly. The intent of the author is only to offer information of a general nature to help you in your quest for emotional and spiritual well-being. In the event you use any of the information in this book for yourself, which is your constitutional right, the author and the publisher assume no responsibility for your actions.

Any people depicted in stock imagery provided by Getty Images are models, and such images are being used for illustrative purposes only.
Certain stock imagery © Getty Images.

Print information available on the last page.

ISBN: 979-8-7652-4725-9 (sc)
ISBN: 979-8-7652-4726-6 (e)

Library of Congress Control Number: 2023921831

Balboa Press rev. date: 12/13/2023

To my teacher, Roger Stainbrook. Grand Master of the Lightning Fire Mountain System of Tibetan Kung Fu, acupuncturist, healer, engineer, man of mystery, bad ass, and the most unique, interesting and kindest person I've ever met. And let me explain kind. Not the bleeding-heart type of kind. Not the kind that gushes over your every word. He was the patient kind – like super patient! The kind who knows we're all connected. The kind that knows the best way to help people is to listen and lead by quiet example. The kind that teaches you how to fish. The kind that never turned away when you said you needed him for anything and I mean anything; whether you had a pain in your back or a pesky allergy, needed the best hug ever, to a swift kick in the ass, company for lunch, a dancing partner, or your car was broken down. You knew you could call Roger. He was that kind. And we are all the better for having known his outrageous love. May all who he touched with this teaching and example be a vessel of the ancient legacy he was a part of.

And so, the ripple continues.

Energy follows thought.

Roger Stainbrook

A NOTE TO THE READER

Welcome to Joy Compass!

First, this book is not therapy nor is it a substitute for the guidance and advice of your health care provider. The reader is advised to consult with their doctor before participating in any of the practices recommended here.

Second, it's important to understand that this book was never intended to be a quick read. It's a combination of story-telling, a workbook and a manual, so take your time plucking through the chapters. Contemplate the prompts. Marinate on your feelings. Experiment with the suggestions and play around with what works for you. After all, experience is our greatest teacher! Seriously... take your time!

Third, community is key with the work you'll do here, and I offer several ways to immerse yourself with a positive and inspiring cohort.

- The book clubs are perfect for folks who have a consistent (or fairly consistent) home yoga practice, but maybe it's gotten stale or boring. If you're hoping for a boost of inspiration and motivation this is a perfect way to stay engaged!
- Folks join our Mentorship programs because they're feeling stuck and are ready to feel joyful and in the driver's seat. Whether you're new to yoga or a seasoned practitioner, it's the most effective way to build sustaining wellness and joy.
- We also offer Nature + Yoga retreats throughout the year in my enchanted mountain town in Taos, NM.

Go to JaymeYoga.com for details.

If you have questions or feedback, I'm always happy to connect with community. Send me an email to jayme@jaymeyoga.com or find me on Instagram at JaymeBYoga.

Make it a great day,

Jayme

ACKNOWLEDGEMENTS

Since 2019 memories, ideas, thoughts, and epiphanies about this book have taken up a very large space in my brain. This is my first book and I had no idea how consuming it would be! A huge thank you to my husband, Doug, my sounding board, muse, and biggest cheerleader. He is a beautiful example of what a dedicated practice looks like and the benefits one receives from having one. I suppose it's annoying holding space for your partner while they are completely consumed with their own thoughts! Babe, thank you for always supporting my ideas, giving me space to explore them and for trusting my instincts.

And Falcon, you dear one, teach me so much! Thank you for making me a mom and for *mostly* respecting a closed office door. Those times when you barged right in for a hug break were always so needed!

And to my dear friend, Beth Kelly, thank for you seeing me in our quick chats and laughs together. Your incredible talent is why this book is enjoyable to read! You ever so beautifully cleared up my rambling, my endless metaphors, and inserted the lighthearted side of my personality into the teachings. I am incredibly proud of this project because I had your guidance and support.

CONTENTS

Layer 3: Fine Tune

Layer 4: Unleash

INTRODUCTION

"One can have no smaller or greater
mastery than mastery of oneself."
— ***Leonardo da Vinci***

When I was young and determined to jam my foot into the door of yoga, I managed a studio and shared my days with Roger, an acupuncturist, a Grand Master Martial Artist and my teacher. I came to the studio each day with enthusiasm and a multitude of technical, spiritual, intellectual, and trivial questions — all of it aimed directly at poor Roger.

For his part, Roger was every bit how you might imagine a true sage to be: Quiet, thoughtful, highly skilled and often bewildering. No matter what I lobbed at Roger, he fielded the inquiry with a stillness that would have been downright frightening if I wasn't such a wild and heedless puppy. Only ever after a most excruciating silence — imagine me reluctantly coming to a sitting position with my tail tucked in — would Roger deliver his answer, which was hardly ever more than an encrypted riddle.

For people pleasers (hand raised!), an exchange with Roger was all at once grueling, awkward, and fascinating. What magic potion did he possess that could keep his head from nodding reassuringly up and down, while listening to someone — and where could I get some?! For the Just-Tell-Me-What-To-Do crowd (hand still raised), Roger was an agonizing marvel to behold. However, for the student on the path to mastery, Roger also offered inspiration and the opportunity to forge a deeper understanding through personal experience.

One afternoon, seeing me frustrated, overwhelmed and complaining, Roger pushed himself away from his desk, leaned back in his chair, let out a big yawn, and in his slow monotone voice, said, "Oooh Jayme, everything is energy and energy is chaotic. It requires a little bit of management every day." I shot back a confused look, which, of course, he never saw — Roger was always disappearing to leave me alone with life's enigmas. Yet on this day, after a few deep breaths and the benefit of being alone with my thoughts, I felt a wave of ease come over me. "Energy is chaos!"

Of course — energy is chaos! — which was exactly the seed Roger had been diligently planting throughout my training, but only on that day had the idea finally sprouted. And only then could I finally see the opportunity I had to shape it.

But boy did that idea still have a lot of growing to do before it would eclipse my dominant mood — the American mood — a disposition rooted in exasperation, stress, overwhelm and an honest to God belief, that feeling massively stressed out was all the evidence the world needed to see how much I loved my job, and, moreover, that I was good at it. Slowly, but surely, and under the steady guidance of Roger, "a-little-bit-a-lot" became my motto.

Another anecdote from Roger that has endured through the years, was the occasion in which my best friend confided to him, after an acupuncture appointment, just how severely she struggled with an addiction to food.

"Roger, I just eat and eat and eat and I can't stop! Is there anything you can do to help me?"

Roger carefully contemplated her question before finally asking, "Have you tried will?"

Oh, how we rolled on the floor recounting that wisdom for years. Will! Will! Have you tried will? Why hadn't we thought of that? Thanks a lot Roger! We roared at our own blaring blind spots: We expected healers to heal; we expected experts to give expert advice; and when we signed up to be fixed, we at least expected some pretense about it! But here was Roger, giving it to us straight, letting us see for ourselves that the truth is (sometimes hilariously) simple.

But sincerely, thanks a lot Roger.

Roger taught the hard lesson, the lesson no one wants to hear: There are no quick-fixes, no panaceas, no life-hack or pro-tip to end all life-hacks and pro-tips. Roger's lesson was always the same: No one can cure you of you. But also, mercifully, the cure lies within.

Well, that wisdom might as well be voodoo for how handily it's dismissed and exchanged for the science of diet, the dogma of discipline or the flash sale on wellness that you can "bundle and save" on with just a few clicks.

Roger's wisdom, and my own slouching towards it, led me to release my most ancient desire: A smoking hot body, of the swimsuit model variety.

Imagine me as a child, in god's country (rural Arkansas), with hands clasped in solemn prayer: Please God let me be skinny, and maybe also very toned, but most definitely looking very fantastic in a red two-piece bathing suit.

Later, as a yoga teacher, the prayer was rebranded as mantra, and buried (but still alive!) within the language of "may the Gods please at least bless me with a defined physique." Yet, the truth was, no matter how I spun it, my feelings of inadequacy had never waned, and all I really wanted was to strut about the place in a two-piece.

So, it was with that image in my heart that I approached my martial arts training. And with due time and effort and practice, I grew to be quite strong and healthy. Only there was no dramatic physical change to my body, and no fix for my morale, which I must have worn on my sleeve, because, finally, one day Roger did say to me, "Jayme, living a healthy balanced life is both science and art."

Once again, my mind split open like a watermelon. All my hedging, all my self-loathing, all my "not good enough" self-talk was what was holding me back, not from a bathing suit, but from joy.

And that's when I began to change — like, actually change. To be truly joyful in my skin, I began to see, I needed to first align my thoughts and energy (chaos!) with my most noble goal: To be healthy and balanced in mind, body, and spirit.

From that point forward, exercise, meditation, nutrition, and manifestation shifted from aspirations — or something I did sporadically and often begrudgingly for conditional results — to just some of the myriad activities I might do throughout any given day for the sheer joy of just feeling really damn good.

I began to approach my subject (me!) with enthusiasm and curiosity, like how I imagine both a scientist and an artist might engage their subject.

The epiphanies were simple, but also nourishing and abundant.

When I feel good, life is good. When feeling good is the driving force, exercising, meditating, and nourishing my body, syncs up with my lifestyle. This alignment eliminates resistance, allowing my new practices, habits and coping mechanisms to become as fluid as brushing my teeth or putting on clothes — only somehow not at all rote.

Outcomes now provide the privileges of health, wellness, abundance and continual transformation. I'm not saying every day is blissful or magical, but rather, even with so many years having passed since I saturated myself in the wisdom of Roger, there's still a trust — a strong undercurrent — that keeps me moving towards that northern locale.

Like the artist who never stops creating, or the scientist who never stops exploring, it is like this too for the master who never stops learning. This is the embodiment of self, and within that embodiment there is no tension, no fight, no struggle or resistance. When you are aligned with the depths of your soul, life is good for you.

And life does of course demand a balance of work, family, friends, finances, health and beyond that, the management of the victories, defeats, mini dramas, major dramas, and the traumas of both the collective and personal. Added to that, most of us still have dreams yet to be realized.

Easy then to see how we may give in to feeling bogged down, angry, jealous or fearful. And also, so very reasonable and relatable to find refuge within the hundreds of distractions that lie at the other end of our fingertips. For so many, it's our dreams that remain on hold, while we stay forever locked in to the cycle of feeling inadequate, dissatisfied and once more lured in to the false hope sold to us on tiny screens.

But what if it isn't life that is so demanding of us? Could it be that we're the demanding ones? And if we're being honest with ourselves, don't we already know it is, of course, actually us doing all that demanding, while also avoiding ourselves, while also holding ourselves to an impossible ideal! It's excruciating, I know, my hand has been raised this whole time!

So, it is my sincerest hope in writing this book that you will begin to nurture yourself — and find your way home to yourself — to reconnect with the joy, love and abundance, which is, and was always, present.

Oh, one more thing Roger says about energy: It follows thought. So, let's go!

CHAPTER 1

My Story

"Human connections are deeply nurtured
in the field of shared story."
—Jean Houston

Before we embark on this journey together, let's first recognize our individual points of reference and how we got to this moment we're now sharing. As a teacher, I've heard many stories of how yogis found yoga, and without fail, it is always said, "rather yoga found me." So, though our circumstances are unique, and some truths are universal, it's our stories that build the bridge we can meet on. Here is mine:

It was Christmas morning, deep in the south, late in the 90's and early in the morning. Mom was absolutely elated — which was her default setting. The woman never held back joy. Imagine for a moment an event that would make the average person happy — like growing a tomato or witnessing the spring lilies blossom. Now imagine Bethel Bushmiaer completely enraptured. Her excitement held no boundaries, it oozed from her pores and sprang from her lips. She was infectious. She was consumed with the magic of nature and God; spending time with her meant you were too. You either loved my mother or you hadn't met her yet.

On this particular Christmas, surrounded by a torrent of crumpled paper from the mass of presents meticulously wrapped for four cherished daughters, it was my mom who was to receive the greatest gift.

After some cajoling from my father, she gingerly opened the envelope marked for her. Her eyes widened. Each daughter leaned in. "What is it

Mom? What?!" She read the note aloud: "Pick where you want to go, and I'll meet you on the first deck!" Then came the squeal. Followed by the scream. And then the flood of happy tears.

Mom set off the Richter scale that morning. But here I was, her youngest child and already seventeen, and I had never once before known my mother to receive anything so extravagant as this promise from her husband scribbled on the inside of a Hallmark card. She was incandescent. It occurred to me, she must have long desired such a gesture without ever having once given it a voice.

Despite their affection for one another, my parents had never taken a single vacation without their children. And I know exactly why — my father was driven by his most noble intentions for our family, our futures. He strove to not only send us to college but to send his future grandchildren as well. He dreamed of helping each of us with down payments on houses, weddings, inheritances, every benefit and every privilege he never knew himself. Every expendable dollar was saved and invested. He was a frugal, but doting husband. And he was a superb dad.

There was only one thing that could puncture the mood that December morning, and no one was talking about it. It was caught in each of our throats — it was Mom's cancer prognosis and Dad's hoping — all our hoping — she would live long enough to board that cruise ship, to stand on the first deck, to let the wind whip her hair every which way, to plant kisses on Dad's cheeks, to bury her face in Dad's shoulder.

By spring she was too weak. And by summer's end she was dead at age fifty-four. Our hearts splintered. Our beloved father Jim Bushmiaer was soon to follow. Leukemia. Three years later. And our hearts shattered.

Each daughter dealt with loss differently. For my part, I questioned everything — planning, trying, dreaming, plotting, saving, religion, the faith they raised me on. My mind and body held so many conflicting feelings and there was hardly a soul who could help me process. I was afraid too. I was sure cancer would come for me.

At twenty, in college and accountable to no one — I had freedoms I could not enjoy. I was slayed by anyone — and I mean anyone! — who appeared carefree or joyful. Everyone had it better. My best friends, strangers, people on TV.

I both resented my friends and desperately clung to them. I felt small and weak when people regarded me as delicate for having lost both my parents. But I also hid behind the excuse when things got messy — when I got messy. Grief was my alibi. It was exhausting. I was exhausted. By the time I finished college I felt old. My joints ached, my moods swung, and I was debauched on every front: physically, mentally, spiritually and emotionally. But, hey, I still knew how to shine on a smile and do an impression of being okay, so when Jennifer Aniston started soapboxing about how yoga changed her body, I thought: Sweet, I'll do yoga, look like Jen and land my Brad Pitt.

Only I met myself. Thank goodness.

Fresh out of college and new to Dallas, I wondered upon this hippy yoga studio that would change everything. My first yoga teacher, Kurt, was super suave. As I stumbled through postures, sweating and shaking, he would weave in messages poetically and almost rap-like, "Let go. You are not what happened to you. Energy follows thought." No one had ever said anything like that to me before. I could feel those hard feelings releasing from my joints, back and shoulders. I began to walk lighter energetically, stronger physically and grounded emotionally. I caught hints of myself — the Before Grief version of myself I thought I had lost.

With time, the sadness began to lift. Something Kurt had said lodged itself inside my mind: "You are not your thoughts, because you can change your thoughts." Truly sad events had transpired, I would never see my parents again, but I didn't have to stay in the sadness forever. Life began to spark again.

And then one day, while driving home from class, for no particular reason, I couldn't stop smiling, and it was my real smile — the one I was born with, the one my parents gave me.

CHAPTER 2

Your Story

"When you know your why, you'll know your way."
—*Michael Hyatt*

So, what's your story?

Where are you on your path to self-mastery? Where did you start? How far have you come? Where have you been set back? When have you surged forward? And who and what has lifted you up? How do you struggle and when do you thrive? How do you cope when your realities and ideals collide? And above all, where are you headed?

Do you feel powerless or powerful? Are you compelled, like me, by the idea that we can best serve the world — our family, friends, neighbors, communities — when we have access to our own personal peace?

We each have gifts in this lifetime — self-mastery is about aligning ourselves and our values with a foundation and process that allow access to our noble goals, greatest potential, truest desires and deep intuition.

I'm thinking now of how we must first put on our own oxygen mask before we can help the passenger next to us. And of course, the old adage: You can't pour from an empty cup!

So, before you continue reading, sit back, let some coins slide down the jukebox slot, turn the old tunes up, and recall your own life's story. Connect the dots how your path winded it's way to here with this desire and curiosity for authentic joy and mastery of self.

4

Tell me who you are and remind yourself along the way. This is the first step to building a personal vision and mission statement.

Think of your vision as where you're going, the ultimate destination. Your mission is what you do every day to get there. Here's an example from a good friend:

> *My vision is that my adult children love, trust and respect me — as I do them. They are happy, and we have a meaningful presence in each other's lives.*
>
> *My mission is to recognize what ails me — to bring it to heel — so I can have a loving, trusting and respectful relationship with my children today.*

Your vision is your inspiration to stay the course should you waver or become distracted (because you will) and the mission will fortify your daily efforts.

Ponder this for a while, or journal if you feel called to do so. This is fluid, your mission or vision may come to you fast, or you may need time to unpack your past and build a vision for the future. If you're feeling overwhelmed, set a boundary, give yourself 15 minutes to think on this and come back to it again later.

You can also start more simply by summing up, in a sentence or two, what you hope to gain from reading this book.

Building connections are not only healing, but also helpful for points of reference. And think about it this way: You can't set up your GPS to get you to a destination if you don't input your starting coordinates.

PART ONE
The Formula

CHAPTER 3

The Formula

*"A champion doesn't become a champion in
the ring, he's merely recognized in the ring. His
becoming happens during his daily routine."*
—Joe Luis

Can we all agree we have to personally experience a concept for it to truly resonate?

Yes, you can be told something 100 times, read it in a meme, share it in a text, and even repeat it to your friends and family as solid advice, but let's be real, none of us ever really get anything.

Until we do.

I was told boys would say many things to get you to sleep with them. But the warnings were just words piled together until I saw some of that for myself on the front lines of my teens.

"Energy follows thought" as Roger said to me so many times made total perfect sense, but it wasn't until I actually harnessed that chaotic energy that I began to truly utilize that wild wisdom.

Partly wanting to please my teachers and the possibility of something magical happening like becoming psychic or levitating, I developed a routine of movement and meditation first thing in the morning. I wanted to be that prestigious person who meditates, but I also trusted their guidance that it was in fact well worth my time.

And so, one morning as I was getting ready for work came that spark, the realization that I had intentionally chose not to put on the - my parents died, I'm supposed to be sad, life is scary and unpredictable - cloak I had been wrapping around myself unintentionally for years. In fact, I realized, that somewhere along my freshly forged yogic path, I had hung it up… and put it back on and hung it up again…and so forth. Not so much intentional but more autopilot. If I felt good, I didn't reach for it and if I felt bad, I did. A thought occurred to me, what if I set my intentions in the morning to just feel good?

Energy follows thought.

I'll give you another example. One day I get a call from my best friend and before I can barely get in a "What's up?" she blurts out, "I can choose to be happy!" I had been trying to explain that to her and I beamed with pride that my words of wisdom had finally landed. She then goes on to explain how she was just at the bank and this bubbly teller was bee-bopping around in a super good mood. My friend commented to her, "Well what awesome thing happened to you today that put you in such a good mood?" And the woman replied, "Nothing really, I just woke and decided to be happy! That's how it works. You just choose to be happy!" My bestie was blown away.

But the thing is Chrissy had been making better choices for her health and well-being for a while and the seed was ready to sprout during that interaction with that bubbly sage of a teller. She now felt it in her body that happiness is a choice. She got it.

This is the process of self-mastery: experimenting and experiencing in order to embody or master.

The embodiment part is the magic. Its literally life changing because you now know in your bones the truth. I see a lot of folks lose that sense of curiosity with personal development and cultivating well-being. So many just want to be told what to do, but that only takes you farther away from your intuition.

If Roger had told me that by meditating in the morning I would stop putting on my "cloak of grief," I would have replied, "What cloak?"

And because I think he knows everything would have then said, "Ok, so I'm wearing a cloak. How do I get it off?" He would have replied, "Meditate."

And then my reason for meditating would have become a mission to remove this cloak I had no idea I even owned in the first place. Can you imagine the frustration when I couldn't get it off? How helpless I would have felt that I couldn't just get over it?

Self-mastery is simply having a keen connection with yourself, your intuition, your soul.

However, self help and self taught intersect when space and time is created for vocabulary, concepts, context, dialogue and debate.

Your teachers, mentors and friends can offer insights, catharsis and motivation. It's critical to surround yourself with people who inspire you to be generous, loving and kind to yourself!

I relish my role as one of your teachers, and I take seriously my responsibility to offer theories and opportunities to discuss your complete wellness; mind, body and spirit. But *you* have to do the experimenting and experiencing. You have to forge the path. You have to fuse the connection. You have to become the expert of You.

The tools you will use include exercise, meditation, breathwork, observation, reflection, envisioning, and intellectual rigor.

Your rewards will be strength and agility, compassion and vigor, nourishment, clarity and actualization of your goals and dreams.

Your practice of mastering your physical, emotional, spiritual and intellectual life will give way to more opportunities to find joy and touch joy when it is present. Just as importantly you'll build an awareness that can also allow you to manage yourself when confronted with chaos, challenge, trauma or any part of your experiences that lie outside of your control.

About Exercise

When a body isn't acknowledged or given the nourishment it needs the mind will become distracted and follow suit. Movement is tied to mental, emotional and spiritual health. Consistent and daily movement, and a lifestyle with built-in opportunities for physical movement is a slippery slope — in the very best way!

The Case for Meditation

Self-mastery requires a ritual of muting distractions, spending time with yourself, and tapping into a curious love for yourself. Mindfulness practices, making time for reflection and meditation all serve to strengthen intuition. Wherever you are in your practice, our work here will provide a glut of opportunities to build a bridge to your inner intuition for meaningful and lasting fulfillment.

True Nourishment

Throughout our time together we will regard nutrition without the implications of diet or restriction. I believe in satisfaction and filling your cup! Our nourishment practice will be rooted in a relationship with *how* you fuel yourself and where you can find more mindfulness within your meals.

The Deal with Manifestation

So much of the practice outlined above is based on observation, but that alone is stagnant. It's when we add vision to our observation that we find propulsion, momentum, expansion, and actualization. This is what Roger meant when he said energy follows thought.

CHAPTER 4

The Koshas: The WHY Behind the Formula

"Movement is life. Life is a process. Improve the quality
of the process and improve the quality of life itself."
—Moshe Feldenkrais

I'm going to circle back now to that part of my story when I first experienced how yoga postures alone could bring not only a physical release, but also an energetic and emotional release. And I want to ask you to also recall a time when you witnessed a change in your own mood or resilience to stress after physical exertion.

Most everyone can intellectually recognize the connection between physical movement and mental health — even if we've come short of pushing through to the full body resonation we alluded to in the previous chapter. But let's not wait for that resonation to don to look further into all the wonders physical movement can also unlock for emotional and spiritual growth.

For more on this, I refer to the koshas, a foundational theory in yoga that guides and fortifies my own understanding of the body, mind, spirit connection.

Within your body, surrounding your Self, soul, inner-being, or conscience (and this is where you'll really want to be sure to use the language that resonates with you) are five koshas, or energetic sheaths or layers that peel back like an onion.

The first kosha layer, the outmost layer is the physical plane or food sheath. In Sanskrit it is called Annamaya. Anna means food. This layer includes all the basic, tangible elements and needs of your physical existence.

The second kosha layer is the energetic sheath called, Pranamaya. Prana means energy or life force. It is this force that allows our body to "tick". Think the systems of the body like digestion, circulation, respiratory and the endocrine and nervous systems.

This second kosha layer also includes chakras and energy channels, which are what acupuncturists attune themselves to when treating ailments. For the most part, without much effort, you can bear witness to your second kosha layer — just as with the physical layer. And likewise, you are also the first to know when that second kosha layer is not firing on all cylinders.

The third kosha layer is called Manamaya. Mana means mind. This sheath is also called the emotional plane, where feelings are housed. Processing our thoughts create feelings. Feelings serve as your body's alarm system.

When positive feelings are experienced the parasympathetic nervous system is triggered, which is critical to your ability (or inability) to rest and digest. Negative feelings trigger your sympathetic nervous system which then initiate fight, flight, freeze, or faint responses in various degrees and intensities.

So, connecting the dots, an easy example would be, when you become angry your breath becomes erratic, your body tenses up, and you react by running away, lashing out, or going into your shell. Intentionally breathing through our anger relaxes the body and curbs the reaction.

The fourth kosha layer finds home in the intellectual sphere or wisdom. Vijnanamaya means knowing in Sanskrit. It goes beyond the mental processing and relies upon internal wisdom – a broader perspective, a deeper understanding.

Finally, the fifth kosha — the innermost layer — Anandamaya or bliss body is what surrounds our soul or inner-being or pure consciousness. Bliss at this layer is beyond what our conditional mind can fathom as just super happy.

This fifth kosha wraps around the Self or in Vedic terms, the Atman, which translates to God-head. The divine light that never goes out which connect each of us to nature, each other, everything around us and God — or Collective Consciousness, Source, Divine Providence or the like. The koshas were described to me as layers of lamp shades around the Soul which is the light.

The bliss body can be tricky to penetrate. You might recognize that connection as a fleeting one. I'm thinking now of the simultaneous thrill and frustration I often experienced in trying to tune my General Electric FM Radio Cassette Player to my favorite station in junior-high.

For yogis, the aim is to tune into the fifth kosha, or bliss body, through the practice of yoga. But yoga isn't for everyone — and it's by no way the only path to a strong signal. I also find solace in the knowing that you don't even need to know about the koshas, or subscribe to the koshas as a philosophy, to achieve the very same essence of connection or peace that comes from having established a frequency with the sublime (or God, Collective Consciousness, Source, Divine Providence or the like.)

For illustration, hold an example in your mind of a time when you felt stressed or anxious and utilized physical movement as a coping mechanism. In other words, you took a walk, a run, checked into the gym, went to yoga or YouTube'd your way through a HIIT cycle while also working through an emotional problem.

You may have started off slow and stiff while your mind continued to chew on whatever it was that was eating you. Soon though, I imagine, your joints warmed up, and your body loosened. Once at a good pace, you started to tune in to your body, albeit it with lots of static at first. Soon however you would have found flow. It wouldn't have taken long for your breath to win out allowing for your physical activity to become the entire focus of your attention.

Your physical exertion gave your mind a chance to become clear — and I'm guessing you remember how good it felt.

Post physical activity, in this universal human experience we're now paying tribute to, I believe you were able to touch, even if for only a moment, a feeling of accomplishment, pride and hopefully too resolution (or simply space) around whatever it was that drove your initial intense feelings.

Movement activates the physical body, which taps the energetic functions of breath and blood and digestion, which in turn generate new feelings, that hop on a call to update the thinking mind, who gets the message and immediately hangs up the phone, in order to extend out the Michaelango-esque finger towards the hand of God.

Or something like that!

No matter how your imagination processes the concept, the point is this: Physical movement is the first landmark on the path to self-mastery. Once this concept truly resonates, you won't be able to unsee physical activity as a deep spiritual practice.

I'm inviting you take the wisdom you already possess — this knowing that even a walk can improve your outlook and go beyond the "I should do that more often" refrain and into the "I do this every day," lifestyle.

Because again, when you feel good, life is good for you.

CHAPTER 5

Practice

"Yoga is 99% experience and 1% theory."
—Pathabi Jois, The Father of Ashtanga Yoga

The joke goes something like this: A Texas couple is driving around New York City on their way to Carnegie Hall for a concert. They get lost, pull over and ask a person experiencing homelessness, "Hey, how do you get to Carnegie Hall?"

And that person replies, "Practice."

Ok, so practice! Another simple answer to a seemingly complex question and most definitely compatible with Roger's philosophy "energy follows thought."

And given self-mastery is a journey and not a contest, there is absolutely no reason to put off building your practice until Monday, or the first of the month, or after the holiday, or your vacation. Start right now. If you are waiting for a specific feeling, or the perfect weather, or a new yoga mat, or the next best-ever workout outfit, you could be waiting a long time.

Begin your practice now.

And sorry (but not actually sorry!) to say, there will be no gold sticker for your effort, no before and after photo and zero certificates meant to commemorate your achievement.

A practice lasts a lifetime. You'll never reach the end — so just forget about perfection. In fact, retire all your measures for perfection.

I like the phrase: A little bit a lot.

A little really does go a long way — but you have to see that for yourself to feel it to be true.

Start with giving yourself a pass to be flexible, to hold your ideas about a practice loosely, to evolve and change with the seasons, to always listen to your own needs. An open mindedness towards your practice may be the only adjustment you need to build and sustain a practice that you come to with curiosity and enthusiasm.

Exercise

If you currently have an exercise routine that brings you joy, keep it up. Pay special attention to what draws you to it. If you have a begrudging routine, or if you later find what once worked is waning, or if you're ready to begin a practice anew, try some of my suggestions below.

Yoga

Anytime you do yoga is an opportunity to combine physical exertion with mindfulness. Like self-mastery, yoga requires you to observe how it feels to be challenged, and the positive effects of conscious breathing and the action of aligning yourself towards support. Emotionally and physically, yoga balances strength and flexibility (which creates mobility) and can help eliminate pesky emotional aches and physical pains.

If you'd like to practice with me, go to
my website JaymeYoga.com

Get outside!

Walk, hike, meander, play, run, hoola-hoop — whatever you like! Do it at the same time every day, or different times. Go outside in rain, sleet, snow, wind. The only requirements are you do go outside, every single day, and that you combine it with movement — for a minimum of half hour. This is the only way to see for yourself the wonders it unlocks for every system of your body. You'll also see nature's transformative spirit is a gateway to meditating.

Whether your time outside is supplemental to, or in addition to, a formal meditation, it will transform another part of your day into a mindfulness practice. But you must actually make an effort to stay mindful. This means no distractions. No podcasts, catching up with friends, texting, conference calls, even music during your dedication to be outside, moving and present.

The challenge is to tune in to your breath, your thoughts and your surroundings. Likewise, the reward is the tune of your breath, your thoughts and your surroundings. Connection.

Mindfulness and Meditation

The goal is to sit in quiet stillness with yourself for at least 15 minutes every day. And it's completely wonderful and something you look forward to. Here's how we get there:

Fifteen minutes of silent sitting.

Studies show that only 13 minutes of meditation can improve mood, stress levels and memory. I've had students ask if a one-minute meditation or just 10 conscious breaths is beneficial. Well, of course it won't hurt matters, but it's active meditation that levels up stress resilience. Sort of like training for a marathon by never running more than one mile.

If you're ready to jump in, set up a dedicated area. Don't overthink it, don't wait until your perfect cushion arrives in the mail. Consider including sentimental objects and memorabilia like photos, books, devotionals, your journal, candles, flowers, whatever feels good to you, but don't make this exercise reliant on building a perfect altar. Again, forget about your ideas of perfection. Set the timer and just connect to the sound of your breath. You do not need to be a statue. Adjust your body as needed.

It is much easier to sit still when your body is loose and relaxed. They say that the ancient gurus invented the yoga postures, in the first place, to assist the practitioner in a quality meditation. Therefore, I highly recommend a little movement first. Keep in mind, there are all kinds of meditation techniques that assist you in tuning in and a lot of fluffy "meditation hacks" to entertain you. Just be aware that you feel tuned in and walk away feeling connected, grounded, inspired, engaged, and clear. Not just relaxed, sleepy or woozy.

I offer 30-minute morning routines on my
website. Go to JaymeYoga.com

Nourishment

The goal of food is to feel satiated, so you can focus on creating and experiencing your abundant, beautiful life! Feelings don't take the time to differentiate. If you feel deprived in one sphere you will feel deprived in others. Abundance can't come from feelings of deprivation, just as an empty kettle cannot pour tea.

Obviously, when it comes to food, what you put in, you get out. Nourishment goes beyond just food to include a mindful and meaningful experience with your meals. Appreciating the aromas, bounty, flavors, and affects will lead to frequent quality choices and enjoyment.

Practice mindful eating.

Connecting to your food through all your senses, brings awareness to how certain foods make you feel. Whether you are cooking your own meal or eating out, take a few centering breaths before you begin. Involve all your senses; touch, smell, see, hear and of course, taste.

In health class, they taught the first step in digestion is chewing, but in Ayurveda (which we will explore later) the first step is to smell your food. This process triggers the digestive system to produce digestive juices for quality absorption.

Start each meal with at least three big whiffs of your whole plate and feel your body react.

Connect to your hunger, take in all the flavors and textures as you chew until evenly spread across your mouth before swallowing. Notice the feeling of satisfaction.

Mono-task! As in, just eat. Bye-bye phone, TV, computer, book, newspaper, magazine, and even heavy conversation. If sharing a meal, keep the conversation light, enjoyable, and positive.

Leave topics like work, politics, money, for later. Best case scenario is to practice mindful eating alone to connect truly to your meal. While chatting with friends is fun, sure, but can you really enjoy your sensations around food like that? I have a fantasy of going back through my life and eat each meal alone, giving it my full attention, so I can relish all the incredible flavors and nourishment that I've had the privilege to consume.

Mindful eating is another way to incorporate mindfulness into your everyday life.

I also highly recommend these practices if you don't do them already...

- Tongue scrape first thing in the morning. Absorbing nutrients properly is the foundation in Ayurveda as this allows the body to function and thrive. The tongue provides a strong tool for diagnosing imbalances. If your tongue is coated with white, brown, yellow or green substance it can mean you have poor digestion, a sluggish liver, or toxins in your gut. By removing the side affect you keep the excess build up from recirculating in your body. Don't worry about diagnosing anything for now. Just scrape.

As soon as you get out of bed before brushing your teeth or drinking water, slide the scraper from back to front across your tongue. Just notice the build-up. Swish some water and spit. Repeat the process until only saliva is left on the scraper. This usually takes 3-4 swipes.

- Drink a cup or 2 of warm to hot water with lemon before consuming food and beverages. This simple morning routine triggers your digestion flushing out left over toxic build up, cleanses the liver, boosts your immune system and balances your body's pH.
- Have your coffee or tea solo. Either drink your coffee or tea alone before you eat breakfast or wait 30-60 minutes after eating. Caffeine is a diuretic, by consuming it while you eat or right after, your nutritious breakfast will pass right through you unabsorbed.
- Stay hydrated. Drinking at least half your weight in ounces is old school but is a great place to start. I've figured out that 80-100 oz is ideal for me. Decaffeinated liquids and broth count. Caffeinated, alcoholic, and high sugar beverages do not count. Warm or room temperature is best for your digestion. Commit to getting half your water intake by lunch. To keep track, use a large container and know how many ounces it holds.

Manifestation

Envisioning is energy following thought towards an ever-expanding life.

I believe manifestation can happen in two ways: Allowing and resisting.

I feel safe saying that we all have a deep desire to experience a life that is blissful, yet we create disruption, challenges, problems and drama rooted in many scenarios like old habits, addictions, and familial and societal rules that we accept as truth, or a trauma triggers us and so forth. But honestly, I think we're just used to simmering in stress (plus everyone else is) and so we've grown to accept that life is hard, and we're not supposed to get exactly what we desire. Our desire may even be coded as greedy or selfish.

The purpose of stress is to keep us alive, well at least that was the case for our ancestors running from wild animals. However, our brain has evolved little sense then, yet we don't experience the same ongoing and sustained life-threatening situations like we used to. So, we've replaced wild animals with mini-dramas and behave as though we're fighting for our lives. So, no wonder then that our simmering anxiousness and big lofty dreams and desires come together to create one hot piping mess!

Your task now is to script what your life can look like five years from now. Consider pondering this during your outdoor mindful movement. This could also be your 15 minutes of silent sitting. Consider the feelings you want for yourself in five years, and then broaden those details from there. This exercise will help pinpoint the values and concepts you need to identify, affirm, and act on now. Open yourself up to the possibilities and paint a vivid picture of what life five years from now looks like. Get detailed. Write about it. Make a vision board. Sing about it. Dance it out. However, you express yourself best, give it the works.

Spend days acting as if all of those values and feelings are a part of your present life. Wear your ideas for the future like a costume. Notice where you feel excited, inspired, joyful, or if maybe anxious, nervous, overwhelmed or ambivalent. Keep editing your vision — find new ways to explore honest, exciting, inspiring, and true-to-you feelings.

CHAPTER 6

Helpful Tips to A Sustainable Practice

On our first visit back to Dallas after we moved to Taos, a friend asked me what my new routine is like. I replied that after I drop Falcon off at school, I drive around the corner to hike where I have spiritual experiences pretty much every time. My friend's father, the sweetest most soft-spoken man, was listening and said with a gentle smile, "Seek and you will find."

Up until then, that saying was a church saying, a song that belted from the lips of out-of-tune white-haired ladies in my childhood church choir. Then it meant, "seek and you will find if the Lord decides to bestow His blessing upon you."

But I finally experienced truth in that old saying.

The first time I curiously stepped onto that trail, I was looking for inspiration, peacefulness and rejuvenation and that's exactly what I found and continue to open myself to receive and uncover after hundreds of visits to that exact same spot. The tone for my day ahead is now set as I'm under in the influence of solutions, not problems. I'm in alignment.

As we all know, a lot of life experiences lie outside of our control. By participating in the formula, you agree to the notion that you are the creator of your experience and by going on that walk or taking time to clear your thoughts you're getting ahead of those curve balls.

Traffic probably doesn't always send you into a tailspin. Occasionally I bet you can find humor in your partner's nagging, your kid's whining, or that hard to please client or co-worker.

Because your reaction varies it's a symptom, more like a signal if you're in alignment or not. The root cause of how you react is what are you under the influence of... solutions or problems?

Ok, let's talk about the ebbs and flows of a typical day. When are you the most alert, creative, and focused? When are you the most challenged or depleted? What most of us find is a natural (or more like nurtured) fluctuation of our mood and energy. Some of us are on a roller coaster. Some of us are just riding little hills up and down. And some of us are on a little of both.

By participating in the formula, you are choosing to get off the roller coaster. Energy is chaotic, but you're in the driver's seat.

Start by adding one part of the formula to your schedule by choosing what sounds the most exciting and intriguing. If you don't have an established exercise routine, I recommend beginning with that because of the domino effect of good stuff from simply moving. However, you might have a wall up with physical exertion, so just go with what sounds fun. The idea is to choose the path of least resistance.

Next get out your calendar and make appointments with yourself. If your day gets easily high-jacked, schedule your new activity before your work flow begins.

Take your time. Start small so you can stay consistent without gassing out. You do not need to be perfect. Dabbling is good. Puttering along is good. Give yourself two to three months to find a bit of a rhythm with the full formula before moving on.

Now, for you sciencey types that like to track results, you'll find a grid on the following pages. Some folks love it, and some find it distracting. It's here for you to use if it helps.

The idea is to give you a bird's-eye-view of your week to see how what you're doing is making you feel. You're looking for a rhythm, and a supportive schedule that you can lean into when you notice you're out of balance. So be sure and mark times, brief descriptions on what you ate and what you did.

The secret to the sauce is knowing how you feel because the whole point of your practice is to feel really damn good! When you feel good, life is good.

"Vibe" is how you feel, and you will rate it with a simple number between 1-5.

1 = You're operating at your lowest self. Common feelings at this level could be fear, grief, depression, powerlessness, unworthiness, rage, hatred, jealousy, insecurity, or guilt.

2 = You're not at your worst, but there is momentum. Common feelings are anger, blame, worry, doubt, disappointment, or discouragement.

3 = You could go either way. Like any trigger and you could spiral down or up. Common feelings are boredom, pessimism, frustration, irritation, impatience, or overwhelm.

4 = You're close to your best self. You feel hopeful, content, optimistic, eager, enthusiastic, passionate, and happy.

5 = You're operating at your best self. Feelings associated at this level are joy, empowerment, love, appreciation, freedom, and wisdom.

Take the grid week to week and these vibe numbers will stand out. Most likely, a pattern will reveal itself.

Let's look at something common like the afternoon slump. Let's say after a week or so you see a lot of 2's or 3's as your afternoon vibe. Start by taking a look at your lunch routine. And also common for a lot of us is skipping lunch, grabbing whatever is available, or a working lunch.

In this case I would opt to prepare a nutritious lunch and practice mindful eating.

I recommend adjusting one thing at a time, so you get a clear read.

My Vibe Grid

DAY	MON	TUES	WED	THU	FRI	SAT	SUN
RISE & VIBE							
BREAK-FAST							
MORNING VIBE							
LUNCH							
AFTERNOON VIBE							
DINNER							
EVENING VIBE							
BED TIME							
EXERCISE							
MEDITATION							
WATER							
OTHER							

PART TWO
The Methodology

JOY COMPASS

CHAPTER 7

How Do I Live A Life of Bliss? An Introduction to the Method

"Blessed are those that adore this life with smiles. They go through the ups and downs of life with absolute love and affection for the creator, for their life, and the creation of personality. Such beings always are acceptable to the kingdom of heaven, which is right now on earth.

May all of us try to be that way. In this life, we have come to clear the account of previous incarnations. In this life, we must add to ourselves the excellence and excellence and excellence. Fortunate are those who have found this formula of excellence. They flow in their life like a river of life and enrich themselves. Anything they touch, pass by and be, they enrich. And may they be blessed, such souls, into and unto their brightness, completion and fulfillment."
Sat Nam
—Guru Jaget

As I drove home from yoga on that pivotal day, (that day when I smiled like an insane person the whole way home, having felt, for the first time, the full potency of my teacher's wisdom — *you are not your thoughts, because you can change your thoughts!* — I knew I would never be the same again.

And so, it was that I embarked on a quest to answer new questions: How can I keep the feeling of wholeness from relenting? How can I live a lifetime of bliss?

Bursting with curiosity I dove headlong into studying, experimenting and experiencing anything and everything yoga or yoga adjacent. I immersed myself in functional mobility, acupuncture, martial arts, meditation, tai chi, Ayurveda, essential oils, reiki… heck, coconut oil, you name it!

I was on fire and I felt a purpose rising up in me, and yet still, before long, my practice wavered, and my enthusiasm plateaued. I was truly disheartened, while also still determined to dig deeper.

When I was honest with myself I could see how so many of my new happy, healthy, vibrant behaviors were still steeped in people-pleasing tendencies, and also maybe yes, a secret fantasy of achieving "guru" status.

I was putting on a wellness performance — and still a long cry from mastery.

Which was baffling! I had tools, wise teachers, inspiring students, a deep library of resources, and even the ability to occasionally tune into my bliss body (the fifth kosha). But those old trappings of people-pleasing and magical thinking were persistent buggers.

One day a mentor asked me what my core values were — I stammered and couldn't answer as succinctly as I would have liked, so I took the assignment home to my journal, determined to take the prompt seriously.

I conjured a vision of myself as an elder, deep in her nineties. I asked her questions like; How do you feel? What do you look like? What had you accomplished? What is most important in your life? And from this inquiry my core values were revealed to me.

Here's what I wrote down: Authenticity; freedom; healthy mind, body and spirit; abundance; connection.

The seed my mentor planted had sprouted. Now that I knew precisely what my values were, the stage was set for my next breakthrough: Alignment.

The mission of my daily practice shifted beyond superficial impulses and toward the true essence of my most noble values. I began to *feel* authentic, free, healthy, abundant, and connected.

Then everything began to change. Every idea I had, every new friend I made, every opportunity I encountered was now an opportunity to align with my values. I was able to test, find, feel, and explore my values with every aspect of my life. And I observed, as a witness to my own life, that alignment attracts fresh ideas, new people and new opportunities for expansion.

Once again: Feeling is believing!

Identifying and affirming core values with all the extensions of your life intrinsically reduces the tension that living in misalignment creates. Yes, it's the living outside of our deepest values — or trying to execute on values we only wished we held — that wears us down and burns us out.

Living in alignment with our values naturally yields a lifestyle that is enriching and enduring. Here lies the path of least resistance.

Of course, this does take practice! And curiosity, an open mind, and perseverance.

The more you learn and experience, the more you'll open, the more ideas will flow, the more desires will awake, which means new opportunities to learn and experiences and so on and so forth.

Self-discovery has no finish line.

Sound exhausting? If so, that could be because you're holding on to an old paradigm, in which your "practice" is a line item you can check off each day.

Loosen that grip.

The path to self-mastery is a winding, fascinating, occasionally treacherous and always unrelenting trek.

You can't speed up on the path, or win the path's good favor, or accommodate the path with your excellent people-pleasing abilities, or placate it, or negotiate with it.

But you can stay the path.

You're not lost. Nor have you ever been. When you identify your values, affirm them and make them actionable, you invite in the experience of alignment and open yourself to the wisdom, grace and nourishment that has been and is always present to all of us.

To help you access these Universal gifts, I've laid out a four-layer methodology in which you will experiment and experience through your formula/practice.

The first layer I call Plug In, as in plug in to You and your energy source. Through reflection and contemplation, you will gain deeper insight into what turns you on. What makes you feel excited and inspired? The goal here is to get clear on your trajectory (where you're headed) and mold your practice so that it adjusts your gaze toward your lighthouse every single day.

The second layer is call Tune In. Remember the days when you had to carefully adjust your radio dial in order to catch the frequency of the station you wanted to hear? And do you remember how some days it was super frustrating and on others it was easy? Energy is chaos, but there are energetic laws in place to help us out. Here we will break down these laws and learn how to manage and balance the chaotic energy from the outside world through your practice, so you can stay the path with greater ease.

And do you remember as you would carefully adjust that radio dial, and the magic moment when you hit the frequency just right and the music was clear as a bell as if your favorite band was playing right there in your living room? **This is what we'll do in the third layer, Fine Tune.** Ayurveda is the science of yoga and we will break down the basics so that you feel connected on all fronts (mind, body, spirit) like never before!

And finally, we get to layer four, **Unleash**. After learning, applying, experimenting and experiencing with all this theory through your practice, you'll find a natural to you flow, space, clarity and confidence to unleash your biggest, most authentic heart-felt desires without hesitation or approval from others.

The reward: The grand view of your life — which has always been right there before you — illuminates.

> Let's pause… How are you doing? Are you learning a lot of new terminology? New ideas? Or am I a new speaker of a message you've heard before? If you're hoping for transformation I highly recommend joining one of our mentorships. There is room for so much dialogue. Go to JaymeYoga.com for details.

Let's continue…

LAYER ONE:

Plug In

CHAPTER 8

Plug In

"Knowing yourself is the beginning of all wisdom"
—Aristotle

The first time I drove a speedboat was awkward — to put it gently. Someone else might actually have called it dangerous at the time. The boat had a steering wheel, so yeah, I did 100 percent expect I could steer it like a car. So, when my friends started yelling at me to veer right, I whipped that wheel like it was my Honda and my friends hung on for dear life. Mercifully laughter ensued, and I happily handed over my boat driving privileges for the day, and I resolved to become a humble student of the boat.

I learned the mechanics of a boat are completely different from that of a car. For starters, the steering wheel connects to the rudder (way back in the rear of the boat) and turns the vessel at its center — so even a slight adjustment to the wheel completely alters the course. Moreover, inertia from the water can push the craft forward or serve as a force of resistance. The idea then, while steering, is not to chart the straightest course, but rather to open your awareness — while also keeping an eye on where you're headed — to find the path of least resistance. Unlike driving a car, you have to hold your idea on how you will get to your destination loosely.

Self-mastery is like steering a boat!

With practice and time, you can relax, feel, look out, and plan ahead with less vigilance. When the process of navigating your inner world becomes fluid, there's more time to enjoy yourself.

Not unlike the mechanism that steers from the center of the ship — when your intentions and desires come from your inner being, there's hardly a need to whip the wheel around for a 180-degree correction. In fact, connection to flow, source, God, inertia — whatever you call the ineffable — is the fuel for a smooth and joyful journey.

Metaphors are everywhere — what speaks to your inner wisdom?

I've laid out four questions that build upon each other — however, if you get stuck, move on to the next prompt. Go at your pace and will and feel free to revisit your answers and thoughts at any time.

Keep your thoughts anywhere that is organic to you, just so long as you dedicate yourself to observing your train of thought and mapping new connections as you forge them. Consider this inquiry part of your daily dose of 15 minutes of mindfulness.

And if you find that this first layer of the methodology, Plug-in, is nothing more than an affirmation of what you already know, allow yourself the privilege of feeling comforted and centered by that.

First, we'll explore what brings you joy because the feeling of joy loosens the grip of trying (trying to accomplish, figure out, understand, change) that sucks out every ounce of fun. Plus, it moves all that heady understanding into your bodily knowing; embodiment. Freedom and ease follow embodiment.

The second prompt provides you an opportunity to voice your greatest life lessons, (or your greatest so far) further releasing you from repetitive not helpful old habits that derail your good intentions today.

The third prompt, which is a major pivotal moment in this book, is uncovering your core values. Core values are your lighthouse.

And lastly, desires. Desires are basically fuel, but this time they will be aligned with who you are and what is most important to your life.

Again, energy follows thought.

CHAPTER 9

Plug into Joy

*"A person must never cease striving to enjoy life. It
takes wit, interest, and energy to be happy."*
—*Kilroy J. Oldster*

Decades after my mother's passing and I'm still in awe of her ability to radiate joy. She was effortless. In quick chats with friends, in the playing of a duet on the piano with her bestie, tucked into quick squeezes or a kiss placed on the cheek of a daughter. Her joy rang out in the planting of flowers and in the easy delight she took in watching her piano students learn to play well.

Contact with individuals like my mother can be startling — an indomitable spirit can even present an affront to anyone armed with a shield to block out the mystery of life, (which my mother could serve as witness to, in even the most mundane of moments).

Some people took time to appreciate her enthusiasm. I imagine they were skeptical, I imagine people wondering if Bethel's effervescence was a facade. But to anyone paying close attention, it was plain to see, her joy was authentic because they could feel it.

When mom died, her divine essence lived on in the hearts of all she touched.

How can some people hold this space of awe — while others struggle to do so. Certainly, everyone has stress and bears the pain of heartache. While also everyone holds the capacity to access the thrill of simply living.

For my mom, her ability to drop into this sacred space seemed to be connected to her commitment to a morning devotional. Most mornings she started her day in her screened-in back porch, which she lovingly adorned with flowers, plants and a simple, but cozy, loveseat.

On the occasion of waking up early, I'd find her there, wrapped in a robe with both a bible and coffee in hand, basking in the peace. I swear now I could see love radiating off of her.

If she ever shared with me any insight to the substance of her morning devotional, I don't recall. And still, I carry with me the abiding peace of having bared witness to my mom in the presence of God.

By giving herself time and space to connect to her energy source, she had an abundance of spirit she could share with dozens of piano students, with her children, her husband, and with the countless people who depend on her to prepare music for church, for sustenance and order, and nourishment.

Without ever using the language of the teacher, and without ever making demands on me as her student, my mother laid down the greatest teachings on mindfulness. She continues to be my greatest teacher. Thanks, Mom!

My question then for you is, where is your happy place? What conditions calm you, ground you, remind and reconnect you to joy, peace, and understanding? What inspires you? How do you gain perspective? What balms allow you access to the goodness that is within you? How do you connect to you, your intuition, your soul?

When you are plugged into You (your inner being) you sit in the presence of the Ineffable — the knowing that you're connected to something bigger than your humanness. This is the sweet spot, the birds-eye-view, the big perspective. I'm certain you've experienced it before. Where all of the sudden you see how your actions will play out, the lessons you need to learn, the understanding you need to nurture, and/or the helpers and teachers placed in your path.

When you can hold this space for yourself, you'll see your ideas about religion, philosophy, science and lifestyle fade. There's no tension in the vocabulary — only peace.

It's important that our how goes beyond philosophy and transaction to feeling and embodiment.

And don't misunderstand me — you'll still encounter unrest, imbalance, stress, challenges and trauma. Self-mastery isn't a path to avoiding the human experience, it is the practice of building resilience, tools and perspective to navigate the full spectrum of human experience with grace.

Now, let's pay attention to what naturally unlocks joy for you. Let's not take for granted our simple pleasures. Let's map these simple joys and watch how this exercise alone yields an abundance of joy. Because actions follow thought. And joy begets joy.

Journal time!

1. List ten activities that bring you joy and take only moments to create. For example, a hug, the acknowledgment of gorgeous weather, a loved one's smile, the softness of the fur on your pet's neck, etc.

2. Imagine ten activities that offer you joy that take a little more effort. For example, exercise, meditation, sex, reading a book, preparing and enjoying a great meal, etc...

3. Visualize ten more activities that bring you joy that require advance planning. Think museum visits, vacations, cultivating a hobby, a special night spent with friends or your lover.

Keep a copy of these lists somewhere you'll see them every day. Memorize these lists! Add to them at will! Then, seek them out and make room for these activities and moments. And when you're afforded the opportunity to enjoy these activities, take conscious effort to breathe in and appreciate these gifts without resistance.

A tip! Snap a mental picture. I picked this up on the television show The Office — which is hilarious! — and I literally go through the motions of holding up an imaginary camera to my face and I manually engage the shudder. Say cheese!

This playful action works to slow me down and turn me on to the present. I have captured so many precious moments this way, and I can return to the joy and ease of these moments by revisiting them anytime I choose.

Through feeling is how we embody. One more note… In case this needs to be said. You are examining *healthy, beneficial* activities that make you feel good and connected, not distracted or an escape mechanism. No activity that you will regret or "pay for" later should be on this list.

Top 10 experiences that bring me joy that only take a few moments…

1. _____

2. _____

3. _____

4. _____

5. _____

6. _____

7. _____

8. _____

9. _____

10. _____

Top 10 experiences that bring me joy that take up to 1 hour…

1. _____

2. _____

3. _____

4. _____

5. _____

6. _____

7. _____

8. _____

9. _____

10. _____

Top 10 experiences that bring me joy that require a little planning ahead...

1. _____

2. _____

3. _____

4. _____

5. _____

6. _____

7. _____

8. _____

9. _____

10. _____

Plug into Joy Through Your Formula

*"Find joy in everything you choose to do.
Every job, relationship, home… it's your
responsibility to love it, or change it."*
—*Chuck Palahniuk*

Exercise:

For a truly sustaining practice, it is absolutely critical that your exercise routine be enjoyable.

If you begrudge it or are uninspired by exercise, return to your top ten lists to see how you can incorporate physical exertion with something you enjoy. If you continue to struggle to make time for daily exercise, then make finding something that moves your body and puts a smile on your face your highest priority and your most noble mission. How's that for an assignment!?

Meditation:

Meditation really is about the path and not the destination. If you're struggling to achieve an ideal you're holding for what meditation looks and feels like — just bring yourself back to the yellow brick road and dive in with curiosity and simply trust the process.

This book offers several journaling opportunities that aim to insert mindfulness and personal time for and with yourself. Use these exercises as investments toward a formal meditation practice.

I've observed over the years that ultra-productive people are the most challenged by meditation. If you're in that camp, give yourself some grace. Rest assured, it's not that you can't, it's just that you haven't cultivated an appreciation for sitting still and doing nothing. The ability to recharge within your stillness is actually a tool for overall productivity. See for yourself — and trust that you can learn to revel in your tranquility.

To that end, set aside fifteen minutes each day until your joy lists are complete. Literally make an appointment with yourself. I highly recommend a morning or evening practice, but for now just set a time that's the most convenient for you. Start your mindfulness time by taking a few grounding breaths. Ask yourself what brings you joy.

Once you have your lists, post them in your meditation space and/or an area in your home where you know you'll see them on a regular basis. Now your 15 minutes of mindfulness will be to meditate on these emerging topics which will plant the seed. There are several ways you could go about this:

Simply repeat the activities you've identified to affirm their importance; or visualize partaking in your preferred activities.

Personally, I find a value in visualizing moments that bring me joy — most acutely when I find myself debauched by the pace life sometimes demands from all of us! This practice of affirming my most joyful moments adds depth to the significance of these moments — fleeting as they sometimes are! — so when I do find myself with the privilege of enjoying that hug or Falcon's laugh, I'm extra inclined to meet the moment with heightened appreciation. And these moments, in turn, become more vivid — and I believe this mindful approach to joyful activities attracts more mindfulness and more joyful opportunities. Seek and you will find.

Nourishment

I'm unapologetic when it comes to enjoying fine details. I love creamy cheeses, big juicy figs, fresh bread, and a fabulous meal. I celebrate with beautiful wine — and I rarely skip dessert.

I don't subscribe to deprivation!

But I also distinguish between mindless indulgence and filling my cup. How to tell the difference? Carelessness always demands a reconciliation. Nourishment does not.

For best outcomes, a good starting point is to inventory your weak spots — those persistent points in our daily lives that leave us vulnerable to impulse and maybe even desperation!

For me, a weak spot looks like my own failure to provision myself with healthy and delicious food throughout the day while I GO GO GO until I'm suddenly on the sidelines of a soccer game starving and scheming to mainline a bag of the team's cheesy puffs to my mouth.

Do nothing more than practice mindful eating before whipping up a new life-changing grocery list. Simply slowing down and inviting more mindfulness in is enough to lead to healthier, more intuitive, eating choices which leads to appreciation. Trust me, that grocery list will naturally improve with ease.

The whole of your being will always lunge towards whatever it is you desire — so the best we can ever do is to change that which we desire. And its mindfulness — not discipline — that is the right tool for the job.

Here's a quick list of considerations to fortify your efforts:

1. Plan meals ahead of time.

2. Slow down. Breath consciously and use your five senses while preparing your meal and before you sit down to eat. Say a blessing of appreciation if that feels good.

3. Set the table. Eat in a peaceful environment. That means no distractions, electronics, or stressful conversations.

Manifestation

Return now to the scripting exercise found in Chapter 6 – where you scripted what your life will look like in 5 years and compare it with your joy lists. I bet you will find several consistencies.

Manifesting your desires with ease requires you taking an active role in simply feeling good. Therefore, actively engaging in activities and connecting to joy will raise your vibration.

What does that mean?

Law of attraction states you will get exactly what you are under the influence of. If you are under the influence of a problem or lack of something, you will continue to receive the problem and/or be hyper aware of whatever it is that is lacking. And how does this make you feel? Frustrated, annoyed, angry, scared, overwhelmed, desperate and so forth – low vibration feelings and the cycle continues.

This reminds of me of what my father would say about finding yourself in a hole, "Stop digging!"

What happens if you are under the influence of solutions?

You just spent quality time reminding yourself what makes you feel good. You also carefully scripted a vision for your future. Through this simple recognition, your gaze pivoted toward solutions and your vibration ticked up a few notches. You might feel content, hopeful, or optimistic just thinking about them.

BUT when you take an active role in engaging in activities that you enjoy especially the ones that connect you to your ideal future, you feel eager, happy, passionate, grateful, empowered, wise, love, and joyful – the highest vibration feelings. And that cycle continues.

Feeling good and slowly working your way up the emotional scale is how you manifest your desires with ease. We will definitely continue to break this down throughout the manual. For now, just let that sink in.

CHAPTER 11

Plug in To Your Greatest Life Lessons

"The past is where you learned the lesson.
The future is where you apply it."
—unknown

My mother shared with me the extraordinary gift of connecting to joy every day and my father modeled for me the importance of intentions and follow through. I learned from Yoga that I am the creator of my experience.

Now, despite having stellar role models, I have absolutely made a lifetime out of creating opportunities to test the validity of these lessons for myself over and over again.

One of the ways I did that — and not by intentional design! — was to seek out the same problems in different settings with different people. Dogs learn tricks faster than me— that's all I'm saying!

But when I've finally learned a lesson — or moved a value I was holding as an aspiration into an actualized value — watch out! It's nothing less than freedom, really.

And as Eleanor Roosevelt famously said: With freedom comes responsibility.

When you've taken the time to identify and affirm your values, there's no going back. If you were to revert to an old behavior, one that no longer fits with a firmly held top value, it wouldn't feel good. You wouldn't feel good. In fact, you might come to feel a discord within your body and mind. I believe this is your authentic self hollering out to say "Hey! We're off our path!"

And when you're aligned with your values, you can always hop back on your path. You may even come to regard forays or challenges as not a departure from your path, but very much your actual route. We'll never stop walking our own personal gauntlet of opportunities to test the strength of our attention.

Examine your own life lessons. Recall a mentor's encouragement. Maybe you got schooled in a random interaction by someone you don't even categorize as "teacher", or a quote from a book or a movie just hit you and you totally got it - you felt the knowing not just in your brain but in your body. Your challenges and successes offer guideposts along the path to self-mastery and that feeling of knowing is your compass.

Your values call you up to your highest self and proclaiming your greatest life lessons is a radical act of self-love and an empowering way to combat the bullshit and tired fears our brains are hardwired to throw relentlessly at us.

As you were reading I'm sure you immediately recalled a lesson or two. Jot them down. Just sit with this question and ideas for a few days. Consider reflecting on this front during your 15-minute silent sessions. You might journal if that's a helpful tool for you to gather your thoughts, or if not just let your mind wander and take a few notes.

As you unlock your wisdom, be present to how these affirmations make you feel.

If you feel inspired, excited, eager, invigorated, empowered – perfect! These are powerful high vibration feelings that lead to positive change on your path.

However, if you notice not so great feelings like judgement, jealousy, discouragement, shame, insecurity, or fear and the like, continue to mull these lessons over. These are low vibration feelings and a hindrance on your path to self-mastery. Consider where your convictions come from. Explore who taught you or modeled these lessons for you and analyze what roles did/ do they play in your life.

Allow me to use myself as an example here. I hold my father in great esteem, so when intention and follow through popped up for me I thought I needed to copy his version which looked a lot like sacrifice in my eyes. Sacrifice doesn't excite me. I begrudge in fact. So, holding that idea around intention and follow through wasn't going to work until I gave myself permission to go about it my own way. Once I gave myself the green light to have fun with intention and follow through doors and windows flung open and I was more than eager to walk through them.

When you feel good, life is good for you.

Integrating lessons learned into your formula...

Find correlations between your greatest lessons and your commitment to exercise, nourishment, mindfulness, and manifesting.

Recognizing when and how you have in fact finally learned a valuable lesson can feel akin to stepping out of a sinking raft and onto a sailboat. And since I'm all in on boating metaphors, I'll say too that life's lessons are the winds to be played to your advantage.

CHAPTER 12

Getting to Know your Core Values

*"My definition of success: When your core
values and self-concept are in harmony
with your daily actions and behaviors."*
—*John Spence*

I think it's fair to assume most people aspire, by the end of their life, to feel satisfied, without regrets, comfortable and surrounded by love. And yet still, so many of us are challenged to end each day like that!

To leave this world satisfied, we must first be so now. Therefore, we have to nurture these feelings in small ways, in simple ways, in everyday things. And of course, consistency is key.

Pay your body, mind and emotions attention and note how you only crave what you feed it. Watch how thirst begets thirst. Sugar begets sugar. Caffeine begets caffeine.

See too how your moods also amplify on their own. Positive attitudes attract other positive attitudes. And, we've all heard the expression, "misery loves company," which of course it does!

Every choice we make today influences tomorrow and so forth. Our habits of thinking, moving, and interacting with life and those around us compounds. I believe it bears repeating: When you feel good, life is good.

Of course, good habits and a positive outlook won't keep challenges or trauma at bay and this whole thing isn't about *not* experiencing them -- but your autonomy of spirit, and your internal alignment, can offer just the perch you need for a bird's-eye view on whatever life throws your way.

Identifying and affirming your core values light the path as well as yield the courage to create the life you so desire. Every time you're outside your comfort zone is an opportunity to practice and test your values. Time spent stretching the limits of your physical, mental, emotional and spiritual aptitude is a solid investment in your future success. The more you practice finding peace in harried conditions, the easier those situations become. Every challenge faced with mindfulness — no matter your level of success — offers an opportunity to grow wiser, stronger and more resilient. New approaches and mindsets forge new pathways and foster new and deeper intimacies with yourself and others. Your world grows and blossoms.

Identifying Your Core Values

Your core values are a lighthouse that set your trajectory to where you want to go. It's as simple of a concept as knowing your destination before heading out on a road trip. And your formula; exercise, mindfulness, nourishment, and manifesting are what you do today to ground yourself (from the ten-thousand-things) so you can see that lighthouse. In a nut shell, simply caring about how you feel and doing something about it is the path to self-mastery.

When you're 90 years old, do you want to be screaming, "OH CRAP!" with frustration, fear, and anger? Or do you want to rejoice, "Alright, I did it!" in satisfaction and contentment? What's important to you? What do you want to learn on this beautiful earth? What do you want to experience? What do you want to accomplish? What do you want to be? But most importantly, *how do you want to feel?*

Feelings are your compass whether you're in alignment or not. And knowing how you want to feel lights the way to what you want to experience.

Below is an exercise meant to evoke feelings that may reveal our deeply held values. This is a big assignment! You may even find it overwhelming. Read through the rest of this section before you begin — and feel free to revisit this exercise again.

Our values evolve as we evolve and develop a more intimate relationship with ourselves. So, you can and will fine tune your core values throughout your life.

Begin the exercise by getting comfortable. *If you're a part of Joy Compass book club or any of our mentorships, you can access the Core Value Guided Meditation. Go to JaymeYoga.com to join.*

Set a timer for about 15 minutes. Close your eyes and focus on your breath. Picture yourself at the end of your life, or as old as you can imagine. You have a beautiful, knowing smile on your face and your eyes are crystal clear — this is exactly who you hoped you would become. You have experienced all that you desired in this life. You left nothing undone or unsaid.

Immerse yourself in this idea until you feel this persona alive within your body.

How does this older version of you feel? Physically? Mentally? Spiritually? Emotionally? Jot down simple, descriptive words.

When the timer goes off, review your notes and clearly state how your older-self feels.

Part 2

Now that you have a clear idea on how your older-self feels, let's explore the tangible aspects of this vision. You may need to set the timer again and go back to this vision. What did you look like? What were you wearing? What were your predominant physical features? Did you pull back the perspective to notice the space or environment? If so, what or who surrounded you?

Then review your notes again and try to match consistencies between your feelings and the tangible aspects of your vision so that a value system is revealed to you.

Core values are typically broad words that evoke feelings + intentions. They're both a noun and a verb because not only do they represent what is most important to you in life they inspire you to go the distance.

My core values are...

CHAPTER 13

Connecting Desire and Purpose

"The starting point of all achievement is desire."
—Napoleon Hill

One of modern life's greatest conveniences has to be GPS. When I head out on a trip and enter my destination I can choose the most direct route or the most scenic route. I can track my progress and adjust to avoid obstacles. How did we get anywhere before GPS? I lived in that pre-GPS world and I still can't fathom it. It's brilliant! So, you know I'm definitely going to talk about navigational tools for the path to self-mastery!

Now that you have mapped your lighthouse/your core values, its time take a look at where you are now and calibrate your route. Start your journey by asking yourself what makes where you are today different than where you want to be? Or try completing the statement, *I desire my life to be right now...* Or, *Things that I wish were different about my life right now.*

Use this prompt as your daily dose of mindfulness for a while. Get comfortable. Breathe. Set your timer for 15 minutes and let your mind ponder the differences between the life you have and the life you desire. Make a list of whatever comes to mind — there are no wrong answers. Setting a timer is a crucial step, no need to stay here longer than that.

If you have over five desires, start with the ones that rank easiest to accomplish, offer the most fun, or the one(s) that you're looking forward to exploring the most. We're looking here for the path of least resistance — which just also happens to be my favorite path to self-mastery!

Five (currently unmet) Desires

1. _____

2. _____

3. _____

4. _____

5. _____

Now review your desires one by one and ask yourself, WHY. Why is this desire meaningful or important? Why you do anything defines your purpose, and your purpose should align with your core values. If you cannot see a direct route from your desire – your purpose – to your core values, find another route or reframe the desire. The work to understand purpose is the goal and the growth opportunity.

Where there is disorder between desires and values there will also be struggle. The tension created between deep core values and desire is precisely what makes some desires seemingly impossible to achieve.

When there is misalignment, our efforts to accomplish the desire will likely fizzle or fade or frazzle us into feelings of not enoughness, or ideas that diminish our worth or drive. I can identify times in my life when I've driven this unsatisfying loop over and over.

When our values and desires are aligned, it feels inspiring and exciting. The path might even be fun and sometimes even, dare I say, easy!

Wherever you are on your map between here and there — or then and now — it's important to foster a deep confidence that there is, absolutely, nothing wrong with you. You are already whole.

The ground I'm staking is this: If you've failed to bring desires to fruition in the past, it may be there's a discord between your deep, (sometimes even hidden) values and your vivid and tangible desires that's not lined up with who you are at your core, you don't get there because deep down, those desires may just not be as important to you as you thought!

It could be that when it comes to desires, we're pretty heavily marketed to. And the truth is, most of us are naturally susceptible to societal desires and visions of success.

I'll have what they're having!

Not unlike the way I lunged towards the image of Jennifer Aniston in a yoga pose. She looks happy, so I'll try that! It worked for her, so why wouldn't it work for me?

Well, what works for other people are reflections of their core values — not necessarily yours!

There is no way to create joy, abundance, and ease when you're aspiring to someone else's values.

Go inward and listen instead to what your inner-being is begging of you.

Review your desires above and answer the question: Which core value does this desire relate to.

1. _____

2. _____

3. _____

4. _____

5. _____

Post this list where you can see them every day. Get active with the most fun and easiest among them. Adjust or add new desires only when you're compelled.

CHAPTER 14

Embodying Your Formula
Plug in Summary

"You are the embodiment of the information you choose to
accept and act upon. To change your circumstances, you
need to change your thinking and subsequent actions."
—Adlin Sinclair

Having identified and affirmed your core values, you may now begin to notice how they shape (or reshape) your mindset around exercising, meditating, nourishment, and manifesting. Now you have a purpose that sustains a life time.

Understanding your stories, your values and what motivates and inspires you is a superpower to be harnessed.

As you continue to grow your relationship with yourself, be sure to stick to the formula and practice of making time for physical activity, mindfulness, healthy and satiating food and drink.

We can talk about theory, philosophy, and ideas till we're blue in the face, but until we actually put this knowledge to use it's just talk - intangible pipe dreams in an invisible world.

The formula is tangible, an opportunity to embody, and can provide solid ground for you to launch these big ideas from.

Continue to look for physical activities that sync with your desires and align with your core values, and likewise for meditation, nourishment and manifestation tactics.

The Plug-In section is a lot to unpack! If you're feeling overwhelmed or unsure, check in about our mentorship programs and book clubs on JaymeYoga.com

LAYER TWO

Tune In

CHAPTER 15

Tune In

"Countless words count less than the silent
balance between yin and yang."
—Laozi

Everything we are, think, see and do is the embodiment and reflection of
energy.

Go ahead, stop what you're doing right now and see for yourself. Your hands,
your clothing, the chair holding you up, the tea cooling nearby, the dog at
your feet.

It's energy's world and we're just living in it.

Both hippies and scientists alike agree on this: vibrations lay not only at
the heart of human consciousness, but of all physical reality. Yes, all objects
vibrate!

Think about that. Everything has a frequency! Now, how do those
vibrations color our realities, our moods, our perception of people,
memories, the five senses, music, money, food, events, pets, environment,
time, and seasons?

And with everyone and everything blaring individual energies and
vibrations, it's easy to imagine the opportunity for energetic chaos to whirl
and expand, evolve, dance, intertwine and perpetually connect us.

Energy is stunning and maddening and all that falls between.

We've all taken that wild ride of good vibes whether it comes by way of a great song, a beautiful day, exciting news, a fabulous workout or a legit victory. It feels good because our level of happiness went up a few notches. And just the same as we make acquaintance with anger, frustration, fear, and anxiety our level happiness lowers a bit and it feels not good.

On top of all that, when confronted with a stressor, our human response (in varying degrees) is fight, flight, freeze or faint – big guns for actual life or death moments, but too big for the regular old grind of endless errands, slow traffic, a poorly worded text and so forth.

Yes, these situations feel like a big deal when they're happening, but truthfully our lives are not being threatened, yet the tricky part is our brain has not caught up with that evolutionary advantage. Getting through traffic does not end with the same huge relief as say out running a wild animal, so for many of us, we keep the hardwired programming and allow life to become a series of stressors.

Perpetual low-grade stress is a societal norm, and its damage to health and well-being can't be understated.

Our physical, mental, emotional and spiritual practice (your formula) is a means to establish and maintain balance.

Balance isn't just keeping your shit together in order to survive.

Balance is a thriving and flourishing ecosystem.

Imagine the world of vibrations coming *to you* — rather than at you. See yourself as you are: the creator of your own experience. Yes, it is absolutely possible to harness this chaotic swirling energy and direct it.

One of the most useful ways I have learned to read, harness, and respond to energy is by understanding its ingredients; yin and yang.

Yin and Yang

Most everyone can identify the <u>Chinese philosophical</u> symbol by its high-contrast balancing of black and white, opposite, but interconnected forces. The black represents yin and white represents yang. But the magic is understanding how these two forces (or vibrations) relate to one another in order to achieve balance.

Energy cannot exist without both, and each part cannot exist without the other. Yin and yang nourish one another. They both keep the other from taking over and destroying all. Their harmonic vibrational relationship is the essence of all that thrives. This high bar of energetic potential is the foundation of eastern medicine.

Yin evokes grounding feelings. Yin is cool, cold, wet, and takes on the shape of its container.

Yang conjures fiery feelings. Yang is warm or hot and definitely dry. Yang transforms and consumes what it touches.

Think of this example: water as yin and fire as yang.

Yin reserves energy; yang expels energy.

Yin is the gas in your boat; yang is your foot on the pedal.

Yin is your savings account; yang is your checking.

Yin is energy that has yet to be revealed; yang is energy unleashed.

Yin listens; yang communicates.

Yin is meditation; yang is prayer.

Yin is introspection; yang is action.

Yin is envisioning; yang is executing.

Yin is resting for tomorrow; yang is seizing the day.

It's easy to see how too much of one force creates imbalance, like a flood or forest fire, spending without saving, binging without purging, too much rest vs too little. And when left unchecked for long periods of time will lead to disaster.

Being able to identify quickly that the energy is off and sensing the right action to restore balance requires your keen awareness. Therefore, an established practice that heightens your awareness is key.

How does it feel when you're balanced?

Yin supports you in feeling cool, calm, and collected. Your listening skills are sharp in that you listen with your whole heart. It puts you in the receiving mode and easily accept compliments, abundance, help, support, and love.

Yang supports you in feeling sharp, focused, determined, and inspired. Expect your ability to communicate and express your needs, desires, thoughts, and feelings to flow easily.

When experiencing a balanced vibration or state of mind, my observation is that I can both plan and execute, envision and create, observe and act, listen and express, rest and engage, receive love and give love.

Feelings of imbalance and how to move the needle...

When yin is over powering, the indications may include sluggishness, lethargy, depression and a heaviness in spirit. Like no matter how much rest you get, it's never enough. Here you need to stoke the fire and ignite yang. What makes you feel alert, active, warm, and engaged?

Signs that yang may be running amok include anxiety, nervousness, irrationality, aggressiveness, anger and hyperactivity. In this case, you need to refill your tank. Think what makes you feel nurtured, grounded, calm, and connected.

In Summary

Too often we wait for things to turn upside down and we're forced to slow down or stop and deal with the imbalance we've created. One of my favorite teachers, Abraham Hicks, explains it something like this… If you're driving 100 miles an hour and hit a tree, it's going to be a much bigger deal than if you're driving 10 or 15 miles an hour. Hitting a tree at that speed will just be a little bump.

This is what your formula is for… an invitation to slow down, pay attention and create ease. The more consistent you are with your formula is how you make that imbalance just a little bump in the road.

Well-being lies within the art of observation and nurturing balance.

What are your signs? Now that you know the characteristics of yin and yang, reflect on how you feel and react when yang is overpowering and when yin is in overdrive.

You might opt to make a quick list for reference later.

CHAPTER 16

Tune into Balance

*"For everyone, wellbeing is a journey. The secret
is committing to that journey and taking those
first steps with hope and belief in yourself."*
—Deepak Chopra

Consistently engaging in your formula (exercise, meditation, nourishment and manifestation) serves as a daily check in and creates a pathway to maintaining balance and well-being. Caring about how you feel aligns you with your core values thus calling you up to right action.

Simply...

- Pay attention. Notice when you feel good and when you feel off. Your body sends signals. Wake up and investigate.
- Plug in. Recall your core values. If you feel off, ask yourself where you have become distracted or disconnected from them. What are you honoring or not honoring?
- Use your antennae. Pick up the frequency and use your intuition to engage (ignite yang) or receive (turn up yin).

When you've identified that you are indeed out of balance, there's one trick that will work every single time, and that is ...Oh right, there is absolutely no one trick. In fact, you're the only person who can unlock your ability to strike balance.

Accept that you are an evolving energetic being. Your needs will evolve as well as your ability to intuit your needs. Self-mastery is the attention you pay to your inner-being. The rewards of living in alignment with your values is the agility and autonomy to be the master of your experience.

A commitment to your formula is your insurance policy against the very reasonable human conditions of confusion, distraction and impatience. It's the antidote to quick fixes. A daily commitment that's ever evolving is the anti-fad diet.

Restoring balance through exercise...

It's easy to classify physical exertion as a super yang activity - spend, expose, expel – like you have to be geared up for that work out. But when aligned with your core values and yin sensibilities, it offers an impactful path to balance. You know that glorious high when you feel grounded *and* invigorated, inspired *and* nourished? You just need to know how excessive yang or yin show up for you and what types of movement stoke your fire or fill your tank.

Allow me to use myself as an example to paint this picture...

Too much yang for me looks like impatience and a hypercritical outlook. I find myself with thoughts like: I'm not appreciated! I have to do everything around here. If I want it done right, I have to do it myself.

When I tune in and find myself red hot, that's my cue to cool off and seek nurturing activities, like a hike or long walk.

Nature puts me into contact with one of my core values; connection and abundance. It's in nature I receive God's presence and love.

When yin is overpowering my senses, I'm in a fog, lost in my thoughts, forgetful, and unaware of my surroundings. This reminds me to engage my attention and connect. Here, and this again is very personal to me, I might opt for a run with a time goal, or a hot yoga class. I need structure, organization and something that will require my full attention to achieve the catharsis of feeling stealth, alive, focused, and accomplished.

On the other hand, my husband, Doug, is a martial artist and an adrenaline junky; intense physical exertion comes naturally to him. In order to feel grateful, connected, calm and grounded, he needs to jump on his bike to blaze down windy dirt roads or check in with his kung fu community by way of sparring. These might sound like intense activities (very yang) but for him they are natural and easy to slip into — this is yin for Doug.

Now when Doug craves yang energy he seeks slower practices like yoga or tai chi, as they require his full attention physically and mentally.

His physical inclinations align perfectly with his core values; adventure and physical strength.

Once again, balance is in the eye of the beholder.

Experiment and experience activities with a mind towards how they make you feel before, during and afterward. Decipher which activities best suit you in times when you need to engage and focus, and movement that feels nourishing and grounding.

You might make a list of activities you haven't tried before but are curious about. Shake your routine up and open yourself to an ever-expanding world of opportunities that align with your values.

Restoring Balance with Meditation...

Conscious breath is a built-in balancing power-tool to feel calm and invigorated, grounded and inspired, clear and connected.

And meditation, like exercise, works much more fluidly without resistance if you can connect your motivation with a core value.

For my part, meditation was sometimes fulfilling while other times something I did because, as a yoga teacher, I'm supposed to. Those ladder times were disheartening. After all, I know fancy techniques, attend workshops, and read countless books to heighten my curiosity. So why the ebb and flow? Then, years ago, I finally admitted to myself how important my relationship with God is and I repurposed meditation as my connection to this lifeline.

Make meditation what you need it to be. Spend time outlining what you want to gain here and find ways to relate your WHY for meditating to your core values.

Use this opportunity to counter whatever energy you are holding. If you come to silent sitting hot off the heels of creating, exploring, or pushing, then consider a meditation rooted in stillness and listening of mind and body. On the contrary, if you have spent substantial time looking inward and receiving, then look to more engaging and expressive practices, like chanting mantras, singing, or prayer.

Restoring Balance with Nourishment...

The body is a very intricate system of energy. In eastern medicine it is believed that all dis-eases originate in the gut, therefore balancing the digestive system is ground zero when it comes to clearing up ailments. We will not cure your ailments here. However, we can plant a seed with some basic and simple information.

In the body, yin energy makes up the fluid and tissues, while the activity or circulation of fluid and substances is considered yang. Nutrients are yin, as metabolized nutrients are yang. Blood and mucus are yin, and the circulation of blood and mucus is yang.

Basic physical clues that yin is in overdrive include inflammation, congestion, constipation, clots, joint pain, and bloating. Here it will help to turn up yang by including warm to hot spices to your diet such as cinnamon, cloves, all the peppers, ginger, turmeric as well as fermented foods like kimchi. Myriad of nutritional experts have compelled me to avoid dairy when overly congested.

Movement that is heat inducing and pumps the lymphatic system is also helpful, like a walk, jog or vinyasa yoga.

Evidence that yang is in overdrive include diarrhea, heat rashes, acid reflux, and indigestion. Think about turning down the heat and opt for cooling spices like cumin, coriander, cardamom, nutmeg, mint, and basil. Swap coffee for green or herbal teas, avoid sugar and alcohol. Colorful root vegetables often prove helpful. Pair these meals with slow moving exercises like a deep stretch, a restorative yoga class, tai chi, or a relaxing walk in nature — anything grounding and soothing with a focus on the breath.

Go easy obsessing over diagnosing everything through the binary of yin and yang. You'll run yourself into circles. Hold the concepts loosely, experiment and keep your attention and mindfulness fluid.

When it comes to your health, always seek guidance from the experts you trust.

Restoring balance through manifestation…

I once worked with a student who was very intimidated to name her core values. She was afraid of choosing wrong, afraid if she named a value it would later change, and maybe above all she worried she'd fail to live up to them. She said, "I just prefer when things come to me and then decide if I want to keep it."

She's certainly not alone in this fear of planning for the future-- its part of the human experience. It sounds nice actually to just wait for things to fall in our lap, see how it feels, and then determine if it's pleasing or unpleasing. But direction and intention are what this ultra-fluid approach is missing. It's too yin.

When you manifest this way, you're more apt to feeling uninspired, confused, lost, unsure, everything sounds good and nothing sounds good. And I would guess more often than not, you get really into one thing and then something else comes along that looks interesting. There's a lot of dabbling.

On the other side of that coin is force – too much yang. Too much jumping, lunging and running down our dreams which gets us into hot messes, off-track and roughed up. Speaking from myself, I want goals met ASAP, a perpetual enthusiastic, overly excited doer and bulldozer.

This is a method for total burn out, frustration, and anxiety often leading to jealousy and anger when the process is slow, or those desires don't come at all.

And so of course, balance is key. You'll want to work on blending and mixing determination with fluidity. Excitement with calm. Thought with action.

The plugging in section you just completed is how you restore balance to the manifestation process. Aligning with your core values, knowing what brings you joy, knowing your life lessons, proclaiming your desires and purpose are all balanced tools to move you forward with ease.

With each realization you are in the receiving and planning mode (yin). And every inspired action is yang. You feel grounded and invigorated, determined and open, calm and inspired. You form connections, make small steps forward, and your intuition guides you along the way. You know you're on the right track because it feels awesome!

To summarize...

Energy is constantly evolving. As you stretch your limitations, become stronger, more resilient, and wiser, so will your formula need to evolve. What was once difficult will become easy. And as you go through challenges, injuries, or illnesses, your formula will need to shift to support that too. You cannot rely on the same practice day in and day out, and you can't trust the ad that says how you're going to feel. You have to try and find out for yourself. *And don't forget to have fun!*

CHAPTER 17

Balance Practicum

"The key to keeping your balance is
knowing when you've lost it."
—Unknown

Your formula is how you experiment with all this heady intellectual knowledge so that you can feel it in your body and discover what works for you. Experience leads to new habits, habits lead to embodiment which leads to mastery.

Play around with the following to explore your knowledge of yin and yang...

Exercise

What does your commitment to movement look like? Do you tend to go with the flow or are you super diligent? Do you wait to feel like exercising or do you have a hard, set schedule? Could you categorize your approach as excessively yin or yang?

To experience balance through exercise, you want to listen to the needs of your body and emotions, but also take authority and point yourself in the direction of your intention.

Try this...

On Sunday, set up your exercise appointments for the week ahead, but just set the time. Then, the night before (for morning exercise folks) or the morning of (for evening peeps) asses how you feel to determine what you should do and/or how to approach your exercise that day in order to restore balance.

Tap into your needs and set your intention.

Meditation

Likewise, on Sunday, establish your silent sitting appointment for the week ahead. I recommend carving out at least 30 minutes so that you can warm up with light movement or you might prefer to read or journal to set the mood. During the warm up you can determine how to approach your meditation. Do you need to listen or express? Observe or envision? Set the timer for at least 13 minutes to simply meditate.

If you need guidance, go to JaymeYoga.com and find out how to access my video library, book clubs or mentorships!

Nourishment

Your urine and stool offer insight to your body's digestive functions. Check out the Bristol Stool Chart online and apply it to your observations.

A food & poop journal can prove helpful to keep track of what foods are working and what areas of your diet may require adjustment. Through observation is how you make natural adjustments without feeling deprived or restricted.

Manifestation

Now that you know your core values and desires, it's time to tune your vibration to that of what you want.

When you take a backseat approach to creation (too yin), you will feel unsatisfied and behind. When you're too aggressive (too yang), you create anxiousness and impatience, neither of which are fun. So of course, the magic is when we're able to do both; hop into the driver's seat + enjoy the ride. You are the creator of your experience after all!

Remember, desires are intangible, a pipe dream, so where we get tripped up is that once we voice a desire we also become hyper aware of its absence and often low vibration feelings like frustration, impatience, fear and the like soon follows. Law of attraction states you will receive what you are tuned into.

Play around with day dreaming.

When you're hit with a desire, spend a little time imagining that you already have it: the job, the cash, the partner, the house, the health, the joy — whatever it is, just try it on for size. Fully live with it so much so that you catch glimpses of what this actualized manifestation feels like to you. Fall asleep with this vision and let your body enjoy the feeling of the experience as you rest.

In this way, you're tuning your vibration to what you actually want and tapping into the joy of the journey. You will naturally gravitate toward action that will bring this desire to fruition as well as remain fluid as things unfold.

Side note -- this is also a great practice to make sure your desires are actually aligned with your core values. While you're daydreaming, pay attention that also high vibration feelings accompany the vision and the experience.

We are creative beings and on the path of self-mastery, we will never be done evolving and thus creating. Accepting that it all truly is about the journey is freeing… and feeling free is fun!

> *Phew! That's a lot to digest! I highly recommend pausing here and playing around with yin yang theory in your formula for a while. Reach out if you have any questions. I love connecting with community!*

LAYER THREE
Fine Tune

JOY COMPASS

CHAPTER 18

Fine Tune

"In 2003, my game was complete. Shooting, defense, using the dribble, transition, mid-range stuff was all there. Then it was about fine-tuning and trying to improve in each area."
—Kobe Bryant

My right eye used to twitch — like a lot. Nearly every facial expression warranted a spastic reaction from my eye. I took to squinting as a means to cover up my oddness.

After my son was born my energy was out of whack and the twitch in my eye got worse. I threw all my energy balancing tricks at it too: smoothies, working out, meditating, juicing, acupuncture, but much to my frustration, my body, mind and emotions never worked their way back to my old self and the twitch kept twitching. I was at a loss!

Then, while out on a run, I came across my friend Christina, an Ayurvedic Specialist, and spontaneously blurted out: "I need your help!" Christina went on to be one of my greatest teachers.

Never underestimate those spontaneous moments of connection that just feel right. The more connected you are with You, the more they will happen. Trust the feeling and the instinct.

Ayurveda is a natural and ancient system of medicine, developed in India over 3000 years ago, based on the principle that dis-ease is caused by imbalance or stress in the consciousness.

Christina came to help me understand that I am a unique individual and that the characteristics of energy is more-broad than simply understanding yin and yang. What worked for you during one season of your life will not work for you in this season of life and the next. And just because everyone raves about smoothies doesn't mean they're awesome for your body. If you want to experience the ease and fluidity of self-mastery, you have to *be* fluid and ease into evolving. Mastery requires fluidity.

She also helped me retire the old lie that our bodies — especially women's bodies — simply "bounce back," after trauma, surgery, an illness or childbirth. After you go through an experience, your body, mind, emotions, and spirit are not the same. But *how* you evolve is completely up to you.

Now that you have a general idea of what it means and feels like to balance yin and yang, we're going to add another layer of philosophy and physiology that is more specific to your personality and nature (your dosha) and explore balance at that level which will fine tune your formula. However, the concepts we'll cover do not begin to even skim the surface of this ancient wisdom.

My intention is to give you more insight into *why* you have resistance here and not there. And to give you a few simple tactics *how* to free up the flow. You're just going to dabble. If you have a lot of A-ha moments and get very inspired by this section, seek out an Ayurvedic specialist after you complete this program.

You can find my specialist, Christina Vargas, at <u>www.simpleveda.com</u>.

CHAPTER 19

Fine Tune: Dosha Basics

"In Ayurveda, our body type or Dosha provide the key to understanding what we are, allowing us to examine and fine tune our diet and lifestyles to create health, strength and energy for life."
—Linda Breatherton

Ayurveda and yoga are two sides of the same coin. Yoga teaches the power of energetic connection and Ayurveda teaches you about the characteristics of energy, *how* to read it, and what to do in order to restore balance and thrive.

Ayurveda is based on three defining energies, or doshas called pitta, vata, and kapha. In Sanskrit dosha translates to "that which can cause problems." Each of the three energies have their own characteristics, and when they are imbalanced, they cause disruption to our well-being and of course, when in balance provide ease and flow to our well-being; you thrive!

Side note here: Roger taught me the principles of Ayurveda through his deep knowledge of Tibetan Medicine – which is quite similar - very early on in our training. However, I would need 15 years to go by before I was ready to absorb this deep well and honestly, I needed a woman's guide. With that said, take your time here. As you accept energy as chaotic and ever changing, layering basic understandings of energetic characteristics offers great vocabulary, heightened awareness, and a compass down the line.

Within Ayurveda teachings it is believed that every individual has their own unique prakriti, or natural constitution – your own fingerprint of the three doshas if you will. And just like your fingerprint is created in the womb, so is your Prakriti.

You know that energy is chaotic, so of course you get off track from your natural ideal state throughout your life. An Ayurvedic specialist will help guide you back to your prakriti through customized nutrition, herbs, and homeopathic remedies.

Let's begin by breaking down the characteristics of each. You will definitely find yourself gravitating toward one or two doshas saying, "That's totally me!" But pay attention to how helpful and necessary *each* are to your wellbeing.

Vata Energy

When you feel inspired, social, and curious, thank the vata dosha! This particular energy helps us to have fun, create, and live life enthusiastically.

The primary function in the body is movement — so it's responsible for keeping the systems of the body ticking like circulation, heart-beat, blood flow, and blinking.

In Sanskrit, vata translates to wind. Its elements are ether and air, so think bubbly, light, and dry therefore its strongest during autumn with the air cool, light and crisp.

The time of day vata is most active is between 2-6 am and 2-6 pm. This means creative projects, collaboration, having fun, daydreaming, coming up with ideas and so forth will be met with the least resistance. You might also relate to insomnia in the wee hours of the morning. Suddenly your bolted awake with a brilliant idea or words and your crystal clear on them.

Folks whose prakriti is dominate vata tend to be artists, entrepreneurs, creators, or inventors. They bounce and prance around light on their feet and talk fast with their hands. My good friend Gregory is totally vata and we used to call him Tigger.

You'll notice that their body and hair are thin and light, their eyes and nose are small and narrow, and their skin tends to be dry.

Pitta Energy

When you have that spark and feel focused, determined, clear in your direction, and able to manage groups of people and/or tasks all while remaining grounded and calm, you can thank pitta energy!

Pitta translates to bile, so its primary function in your body is to create heat to metabolize, digest, absorb nutrients and regulate temperature.

Its elements are water and fire and is the only dosha that can strike a balance between two polarities, a spark but it's not burning out of control. With heat being its main characteristic, it is the most-strong during the Summer months.

Pitta energy is most active between 10a - 2p and 10p - 2a. This is the midmorning fire that helps you burn through your day's chores. Ayurveda recommends lunch be your biggest meal as your digestive fire is the strongest between 11a – 1p. You might also relate to that 10 pm second wind of energy or late-night hunger that keeps you up past your bedtime. However, this second wave is to help you digest left over food, emotion and stress from the day, not overload your system. The optimal time to be in bed is 9:45p so that you are resting and recovering.

Folks whose prakriti is dominate pitta, are intelligent, energetic, determined, focused, grounded, goal-oriented, and passionate. Managers, CEOs, leaders, directors, guides, and teachers are usually pitta dominate.

You might notice that physically speaking they are a happy medium. They gain and lose weight easily and have good musculature, medium-sized eyes, lips and nose, hair is not too thick or thin, and skin is balanced.

Kapha Energy

When you feel patient, loving, empathetic and kind, you can thank kapha energy. As the nurturer of the three, it supports our ability to truly connect with ourselves and others.

Kapha translates to phlegm and its primary function in your body is nourishment. It is responsible for soft organs and lubricating and maintaining moisture.

With the elements of earth and water, it is strongest in the winter and spring.

The time of day kapha is most active is between 6 - 10a and 6 -10p. With its role as the nourisher and connecter, it supports an early morning self-care routine as well as quality time with yourself or loved one(s) in the evening. You might also relate to feeling super slugging in the morning.

Dominate kapha types are wonderful listeners, thoughtful, grounded, and empathetic. Unconditional love comes very easy to them and they thrive in a 1:1 setting. Expect caregivers, counselors, therapists, and doctors to be kapha dominate.

You might notice that they have a strong bones and musculature, thick and shiny hair and skin, full lips, large eyes, and a wide nose.

In summary...

As creative beings we need a range of energy themes to thrive. Vata provides the enthusiasm and movement, pitta gives us the fire to follows through, and kapha keeps us together in a loving way.

Of course, dosha means "that which can go wrong" so let's keep digging and discover what these energies look and feel like when out of balance. But before you read on, it's a good time to discover your prakriti! You can find lots of free dosha quizzes online. Keep in mind, an online survey will not be as thorough as a specialist.

After you discover your dosha, reread this chapter again and continue on to the next chapter.

CHAPTER 20

Fine Tuning the Doshas

"Your body is precious. It is our vehicle for
awakening. Treat it with care."
—*Buddha*

You now know that balance is about finding harmony between what has become too loud and what has become too quiet.

We all unconsciously (and also consciously) pick up our groceries with the dominate arm because we know it can handle it. And in this universal experience, you've probably found yourself in the physical therapist or chiropractor's office where they sincerely try to motivate you to use your core, consciously pick up your stuff with your other arm, or hold the baby on the other hip...etc. They're trying to get you to quiet the overly used strong muscles and wake up the muscles you're not utilizing in order to create a harmonious musculature relationship thus eliminating pesky aches and pains brought on from imbalance of use.

When it comes to harmonizing your doshas, the same principle applies.

Your dominant dosha will want to be the muscle while your weaker one(s) is continuously over powered.

Seasons will also exasperate side effects as well as the time of day the dosha is most active.

Let's take a look at what can go wrong when a dosha is too strong.

Vata...

Your head is in the clouds and you're bouncing and flitting about in quick jerky motion. You can't focus on who or what is in front you, and you feel like you're just running in circles. Communication is difficult because your thoughts are all in your head.

Anxiousness, fear and insecurity are dominating your emotions and you might try to conceal it by talking and moving fast with boisterous expressions.

Forgetting to eat, inability to gain weight, dry stools, constipation, eczema, insomnia, hyper-tension and bodily twitches are physical clues.

Between the hours of 2-6AM you experience intense insomnia. Anxiousness, worry and fear bolt you awake. I notice this happening to me when I'm going through change, even good change like when Falcon was an infant. As a new mom I would wake up at 3AM with intense worry that something terrible was going to happen to us.

If you're prakriti is dominate vata then most of the above will sound very familiar to you. If you are not dominate vata, you might pick out a few signs that are common to you. For example, my eye twitch and insomnia anxiety are always a big clue for me that vata is becoming too strong.

Reread the above section and highlight your "that's me" moments.

Balancing Vata energy through your formula...

Because vata's nature is upward moving (ether and air) it makes sense that when it's too strong it can send you floating away. Therefore, you want to induce stability, calm, connection, and focus and reduce over stimulation.

Exercise... You will need intensity to grab your attention, vigor to get out the wiggles and a warmth to soothe the nerves.

A led class like at a gym or studio might be necessary to take the pressure off of leading yourself but make sure the community, environment and teaching style help you focus and connect to You – mind, body, and spirit. Once you're in the groove, you might opt for self-led exercise sessions like a run, vigorous walk, or HIIT class, but again make sure your environment is grounding and the music (if you choose) induces focus and connection to your breath and rhythm. For example, my go to is a vigorous hike or a timed run in the mountains. The intensity and the terrain force me to focus, no music helps me be truly present to the surrounding nature and my phone is definitely on silent.

Exercise before you work day begins. Not only will you feel accomplished, but that grounded and focused energy will carry over into your day.

Mindfulness & Meditation... A morning routine before you work day begins and during kapha hours (6-10am) will support connection. Set your alarm 45 minutes early so you're not rushed. Warm-up the room and begin with grounding activities like gentle stretching or journaling. Guided meditations will help hold the space for you. On my site check out the Mountain Meditation, Yoga Nidra, and tapping.

Finish by making a short to-do list of things that would feel really good to complete that day. They should only fit on a post it-note. Do them between 10a-2p.

An evening routine to prepare for sleep helps reduce insomnia. Nurture your body with coconut oil or soak in an oil bath with sweet essential oils like lavender, ylang ylang, jasmine, sweet orange, rose, and sandalwood.

Keep a journal or notebook by your bed to release that sticky thought or worry that's causing your insomnia.

Also pay attention to the people in your life and settings that are over stimulating and cause distraction, this includes social media, the news, and TV shows. You will need to limit your exposure until you're recharged.

Nourishment... Schedule eating times and practice mindful eating. Avoid over stimulating foods like sugar and caffeine. Reach for sweet, sour and salty tastes. Use coconut oil or ghee and spices like fennel, cinnamon, cardamom, turmeric, ginger, black pepper and dill. Opt for moist and warm and dishes.

Manifestation... Observation + envisioning = dreams realized. And of course, you now know that *energy follows thought*. The problem with out of balance vata is the envisioning and too many thoughts part. You need to ground your ideas and dreams into small tangible steps forward.

For this I use what I call a "bubble to-do". I take out a few sheets of paper and label a category on each sheet, like "home improvements" or "Jayme Davis Yoga". In no particular order I jot down ideas that have been on my mind, things I'd like to do, or stuff I'd like to see come to fruition. I only let myself write down 5 things to keep it simple. Then under each item I jot down what I could actually do *that day* to get to the ball rolling. So, let's say I really want to renovate my bathroom. I've been drooling on Dwell's Instagram feed for months but I'm not going to get that bathroom until I put to pen to paper on the materials I want and the costs. So, "research bad-ass bathroom fixtures" would be on that to do.

Next when you find yourself bored, distracted, or wasting time fiddling around, pull out your sheets and pick one to-do that sounds fun and dig in!

Pitta

Too much fire can set the world aflame and a pitta temper can come out of nowhere. Your focus is razor sharp, so sharp that you might cut someone standing in your way. Highly competitive, you are often crippled by jealousy. Angry, irritable, and annoyed are your default setting.

Physically, hunger and thirst can be insatiable. You run hot. Look for stool that is loose to watery as well as ulcers, rashes, heart burn and indigestion.

At 10PM your second wind is all consuming. Reorganizing your closet, deep cleaning your kitchen, and/or hunger that could clear out your pantry and fridge are big clues.

For those whose prakriti is dominate pitta (me!) you probably had your hand raised the whole time! For everyone else, a few may have stood out. Check off a few signs for you that pitta energy is becoming too strong.

Balancing pitta through your formula...

The good news is that pitta's elements are balanced, fire and water, so it doesn't take much to chill it out. It's the fire part that gets out of control – so think turn down the heat, loosen up and have some fun.

Exercise... You'll need to pay attention to what sparks your competitive nature and either avoid the environment all together for a bit or try to set your intention before-hand to just have fun. Also avoid hot settings and the hottest time of day especially in the summer. Don't exercise on your lunch break.

Sometimes when that aggressive nature is boiling up, we need intensity to channel it out, so forcing yourself to do something like restorative yoga right off the bat will be annoying. Ease into it. Put down the timers, the goal and just set out for a nice walk outside, a slow jog or a bike ride. Take someone fun along with you.

Once you're in a groove, pittas need to carve out time on their schedule for cooling exercises about once a week; like tai chi, restorative yoga, deep stretch, relaxing walks, etc.

Mindfulness & Meditation... A morning routine (during kapha hours) that is nurturing, relaxing and grounding. Begin with gentle stretches or the foam roller to loosen up tight muscles. Then shift into meditations that involve appreciation, cooling breath techniques like alternate nose breathing, or guided meditations like yoga nidra.

An evening ritual might prove critical to set down the day and prepare for sleep. Use a warm oil bath with chamomile and lavender + herbal teas. Start this process no later than 9pm and be in bed by 9:30p so that you are asleep before pitta's second wave begins.

Pay attention to people, settings and activities that cause you to feel competitive, jealous, angry and/or irritable. You may need to limit your exposure until you're more balanced.

Nourishment... Meal plan + schedule your meals ahead of time. Include nourishing snacks to have on hand so that you're not grabbing whatever is in front of you. Practice mindful eating and give a blessing or meal appreciation before you eat. Stay hydrated.

Enjoy cooked foods in coconut oil or ghee that are salty and sweet with cooling spices like cumin, coriander, cardamom, fennel, nutmeg, mint, basil, turmeric. Avoid spicy, hot, dry, raw, and fermented foods as well as alcohol, sugar and caffeine as these are heat inducing in your gut.

Eat your biggest meal with protein during 11a-1p.

Manifestation... The trouble with manifesting your desires when pitta is running on high, is impatience, lack of trust, and forcing the ball forward. You need to lighten up and remember that creating is fun! Go back to your joy lists and make room for them throughout the day.

Kapha...

You feel stuck, tired, and depressed. It doesn't matter how much rest you get, it's never enough. It's easy for you to develop an unhealthy attachment to outcomes and people through control or manipulation. You might also struggle with feelings of envy, insecurity and inflexibility.

In the body, it can show up as weight gain, excessive congestion, water retention, and stiff and sore joints. Other symptoms could be difficulty to pass bowel movements, diabetes and/or obesity.

You have the most trouble getting out of bed in the morning, especially if you sleep past 6am and the thought of working out or a self-care routine sounds completely impossible.

Again, kapha dominate types will resonate with most if not all of the above. When kapha is getting out whack for me it shows up as congestion, weight gain and sore joints. Check off your clues!

Balancing kapha through your formula…

With the elements of water and earth, the goal is to stoke the fire and get moving.

Exercise… You'll want to get engaged with a fun and inspiring community. Honestly, I think dancing is the best for kapha dominates but also a really positive running group, cycling club, yoga community and the like is wonderful! You need vigorous, upward moving, heat inducing movement. Be aware of settings and environments that feel rigid or strict to you.

Do your exercise before 9AM to offset sluggish kapha energy.

Mindfulness & Meditation… Lethargic kapha needs to be kicked to the curb first thing when you wake up. I recommend a 5am alarm so that you utilize bubbly vata. Grab a hot green tea, head into a warm room and opt for lymphatic pumping movement… arm rotations, waists twists, hip rotations, jumping jacks, jump rope…heck, hop on a trampoline!

You might also like to listen to an inspiring podcast, uplifting music, or a motivational speaker you love.

Choose meditations that involve chanting, prayer, singing or firey breathing techniques.

Of course, you have to head to bed early if you're going to wake up at 5am, and to help you prepare for sleep a hot bath with Epsom salt is best to counter inflammation.

Nourishment… Caffeine in the morning is fine for kaphas. Eat cooked food with pungent, bitter, and astringent tastes. Use light oils and spice it up with cloves, cinnamon, ginger and all the peppers. Fermented foods are good too!

An after-dinner walk is great for kaphas to help induce digestion.

Manifestation... When kapha is super strong it's the envisioning and energy part that will fade away. You want to keep a list of books, speakers, artists, music, settings, your joy lists that really spark your curiosity and inspiration. Kaphas need to make time on their schedule to regularly engage with fun and curiosity.

The bubble diagram I described in the vata manifestation section is also great for kaphas. But the idea is more about engaging in fun in order to eliminate resistance and stagnation. Kapha types tend to get stuck in the "I have to" or "it's expected of me" ...screw that! Life is supposed to be fun!

In summary... Start by pacifying or balancing your dominate dosha and know that as you do that you're strengthening your weaker one(s). Try not to over diagnose. As you read through, check mark a few things and practices that make sense to you and start experimenting so you can experience if it's right for you.

CHAPTER 21

Fine Tune Your Schedule

*"The great thing about Ayurveda is that its treatments
always yield side benefits, not side effects."*
—*Shubhra Krishan*

One of my big missions in writing this manual is to help you establish a flow
and rhythm in order to invite room for ease, joy and growth. Of course, we
use schedules and book appointments every day as a way to establish space
for important stuff like meetings and doctor's visits, and so the same theory
works for our personal development and aligning with our core values in
order to experience the life we were born to live. What's more important
than that?! We simply have to get out ahead of it like we do everything else.

On the following page is a sample schedule that uses the strengths of each
dosha to your benefit. The more balanced and in tune you are with your
well-being the more you will be able to feel this under current of support.

You won't use this schedule day in and day out, but you'll find it greatly
beneficial to pick and choose practices that work for you according to your
needs. And in order to do that you have to experiment with and experience
it for yourself.

You are the only person that knows exactly what you need. But here are a
few tips to experiment with to get started…

…Take the dosha quiz if you haven't already. Familiarize yourself with your
dosha's strengths and weaknesses and contemplate how they show up in
your experience.

...Remember your dominate dosha will typically want to be the muscle so, start by exploring methods to counter or soften over stimulation.

...Check out the schedule to figure out the best time this counter practice is the most supported.

...Pay attention to feeling overwhelmed and back off if needed but also accept that a change in your schedule takes time to acclimate to. So again, we have to listen + guide ourselves.

The Ayurvedic Schedule

5:30 AM Wake Up Do...	Get in front of sluggish kapha energy. Grab your hot water w/lemon, tongue scrape and oil pull
6 AM - 10 AM Kapha Time Do...	...a balanced morning routine. ...exercise especially for kapha and pitta dominate types. ...eat a warm light breakfast. ...prepare for your day mentally and emotionally.
10 AM - 2 PM Pitta Time Do...	...knock out your to do list. ...eat your biggest meal between 11AM - 1PM and practice mindful eating. ...pay attention to over stimulation like competitive exercise especially for pittas.
2 - 6 PM Vata Time Do...	...schedule collaborative meetings, goal set, day dream and creative projects. ...refer to your joy lists to spark inspiration and fun. ...fun and grounding exercises.
6 - 10 PM Kapha Time Do...	...connect to yourself and/or loved ones. ...nourishing to you exercise. ...eat a light dinner and practice mindful eating. ...a relaxing walk to connect and aid digestion, great for kapha dominates. ...prepare for sleep with an evening ritual - meditation or other mindfulness practices, bathing, herbal teas, etc. ...be in bed by 9:30 or 9:45 PM
10 PM - 2 AM Pitta Time Do...	...rest. Your body is processing undigested food and mental and emotional stress left over from the day. Let your body recover.
2 AM - 6 AM Vata Time	Vivid dreams and insomnia from bright ideas and/or worry are common at this time. Develop a way to release those sticky thoughts so you can get back to sleep. A notebook or journal by your bed might be helpful. The closer you get to 5'ish AM, just get up and accept that you'll probably be tired that afternoon and may need a nap.

CHAPTER 22

Ayurveda Cliff Notes

*"Because we cannot scrub our inner body we need
to learn a few skills to help cleanse our tissues,
organs, and mind. This is the art of Ayurveda."*
—Sabastian Pole

Below is an over view of some of the most important practices and methodologies in Ayurveda. My intention is that you have an opportunity to try it on. As I mentioned earlier, the best and most effective way to benefit from this lifestyle is to have a guided practitioner to help you customize your needs. If you're experiencing a pesky, long-term ailment, do not try to self-diagnose. Seek the guidance of an expert. My practitioner is Christina Vargas of SimpleVeda.com. I love her recipes too!

Scrape your tongue first thing in the morning. Absorbing nutrients properly is the foundation in Ayurveda as this allows the body to function and thrive. Scraping the tongue removes problematic bacteria from undigested food and stress. The tongue also provides a strong tool for diagnosing imbalances. Jump online and look up Ayurvedic tongue diagnostics you'll find insightful information about your digestion by simply observing your tongue. A practitioner will help you understand this even better.

After tongue scraping, oil pull. Put a spoonful of coconut oil in your mouth, let it melt down and swish in your mouth and between your teeth for about 15 minutes. Coconut oil has been used for centuries as an effective oral hygiene practice. Current research suggests it may reduce bad bacteria, prevent gingivitis, tooth decay and get rid of bad breath – it's also a natural way to whiten your teeth.

After oil pulling, drink hot water with lemon. Which we started doing at the beginning of the course. It aids in digestion as it balances the body's pH, removes toxins from the gut, and promotes bile production. Plus, the extra boost of vitamin C is great for your immune and nervous system.

Opt for room temperature to warm water throughout the day. Again, it's all about the digestion and ice-cold drinks put out the digestive fires.

What does your stool tell you about the quality of your digestion? Digestion is the central key in Ayurveda, as is in all eastern medicine, and is believed that all dis-ease starts in the gut, and all cures lie there as well.

Western medicine is finally coming around to this simple fact too. Food is, of course, medicine. It can also be poison.

Check out the Bristol Stool Chart online if you haven't already and spend a few weeks observing your movements.

Keeping a poop journal was my first assignment when I started working with Christina. Before that experience I thought having a bowel movement 2-3 times a day was a good sign, however what I learned via my Ayurvedic education is that my bowel movements reflected how poorly I was absorbing nutrients, which attributed to my twitching eye and difficulty losing excessive weight.

Eat in a peaceful environment or what they say in Ayurveda, a saatvic environment. Because digestion is the central key, how you consume food, not just what you're consuming, is worthy of your attention.

Practice mindful eating by preparing the table for a meal and eliminating distractions. Avoid stressful topics like politics, money or problems to be solved. In fact, when possible, eat in silence!

Whether you're talking about stressful topics, watching a stressful movie, or listening to stressful information on the news, your body and emotions still goes through the same fight, flight, freeze, or faint reaction – just less so compared to when you're actually in front of said stress. Digesting food requires a lot of energy, yet our brain is hard-wired to protect us first. So, if you're eating while simmering in stress, the energy you need for digesting will be redirected to your natural reactionary response. The side effects will be gas, bloating, indigestion, heart burn, and/or diarrhea.

Look at your plate of food and take in the colors, bounty, and aroma. Give space for appreciation of the process your food went through to arrive on your plate. Take three whiffs to notice the feeling of hunger. It is believed that smelling your food is actually the first step in digestion as your body begins producing digestive juices. Chew your food and take in all the flavors and textures until it is evenly spread in your mouth, and then swallow, connecting to the satisfaction when it hits your stomach. There really is no way you can do that while carrying on a conversation.

Eat food that is cooked and full of flavor. Ayurveda does not agree with the raw food movement. Food is cooked with your doshic appropriate heat, oil, and spice to ensure optimal absorption of the food's medicine.

Opt for grains paired with veggies, or proteins and veggies but skip proteins with grains. Again, it's all about digestion. Completely digesting protein can take between 3 - 6 hours, grains 1 - 3 hours, veggies under an hour, and fruit within 30 minutes. The idea is to not overload the system. Digesting our food requires the most energy — another reason why late-night eating does not make for quality sleep.

Fruit is not dessert and should be consumed alone. Raw fruit is digested in about 30 minutes and when consumed right after a meal will act as a diuretic. So, let's say you enjoy a nice steak dinner and opt for strawberries for dessert. The steak needs about 4-6 hours to digest and if you add berries to the top, it will sit for hours fermenting and creating gas. Ayurveda recommends raw fruit be enjoyed alone and preferably an hour before eating a meal, not after. Cooked fruit with oil and spice is the exception to the rule. Keep in mind, *any* sugar or caffeine sitting on top of a heavy meal, especially meat, will ferment and work like a diuretic.

Ghee. Ghee is life! Ayurveda recommends several types of cooking oil, but ghee is definitely the favorite. Ghee is nothing other than butter that has gone through a heating process to remove moisture and separate milk solids to be strained out. It is the beautiful golden sun yellow nutty buttery-tasting trans-fat that makes everything amazing (if you ask me). It is a high heat oil, anti-inflammatory, immune boosting, cell-rejuvenating, joint lubricating goodness. You can make ghee yourself with quality unsalted butter. There are lots of videos online to walk you through the process.

Spice. Spice is another way to aid in digestion but knowing your dosha is essential.

Kapha dominant doshas should opt for pungent spices like pepper, mustard seeds, ginger, cloves, and cayenne.

Vata dominant doshas should reach for sweet, salty and sour spices like cardamom, cumin, ginger, cinnamon, salt, cloves, mustard seed and fennel.

Pitta dominate doshas go for more sweet tastes like basil, coriander, occasionally black pepper, ginger, fennel, mint, orange peel, saffron, peppermint, occasionally cinnamon, dill, cardamom, parsley and vanilla.

Grains and beans should be soaked, preferably over-night or at least for a few hours with a pinch of salt and lemon or vinegar. This will release the external coating for easier digestion. It also helps to speed up the cooking process.

When cooking, allow the veggies, grain, or protein to soak up the oils and spice before adding any liquid that way all the good stuff that helps you break down nutrients are soaked into your food.

LAYER FOUR
Unleash

JOY COMPASS

CHAPTER 23

Unleash

"The Law of Attraction states that whatever you focus
on, think about, read about, and talk about intensely,
you're going to attract more of into your life."
—Jack Canfield

My friend Rich is naturally joyous. Rich is always quick to share a story of how some challenge or adversity worked out perfectly in the end. A common refrain from Rich is, "The universe just lined up!"

Recently Rich was driving in the middle of Nowhere, New Mexico, when suddenly every warning light on his dash flipped out. He found a mechanic to run a diagnostic and was relieved to find out that just a simple part needed replacing, only there was no mechanic in the area to do it.

But just as he learned this news, someone overheard the prognosis, and low and behold, they owned a shop nearby where the fix could be made.

Once again Rich noted, "Things just worked out, and I even made a new friend!"

For folks like Rich, who for the most part maneuver through life feeling joyful — a very high vibration — things typically *just* work out. He's curious and expects the best of people, so he typically attracts good people. Because he generally feels good, life is generally good to him. Even if no mechanic happened upon his crisis, I suspect Rich would have ultimately ended this saga with the same sentiment: "It all just worked out perfectly". Yes, he would have been stressed, but he wouldn't dwell and would have found a way to approach the dilemma with curiosity and a new experience.

The Rich's of the world are in the habit of non-resistant thought. Meaning they don't resist what it is. Of course, no one is happy about a broken-down car, but they quickly slide into the flow, take right action, trust, and expect the best. High vibration feelings like faith, in this example, create more non-resistant thoughts which place Rich in the receiving mode of his needs and desires.

And of course, we have the opposite end of the spectrum. We have all witnessed the trials and tribulations of those so inclined to encounter trials and tribulations.

Resistant thoughts find beef with reality and are based in fear and separateness. Car trouble on a road trip is a traumatic experience so much so that they may think the Universe is against them or testing them. These low vibration feelings do not match the high vibration of their desires and needs, therefore, according to Law of Attraction, they can't receive them.

Reading the above, I'm sure you recalled times when you were in resistant thought and nonresistant thought. This isn't about resistant thought being good and nonresistant thought being bad or that we should all desire to be happy go lucky all the time. Rather my intention is for you to reflect on which direction do you naturally gravitate toward.

Knowing your starting coordinates is the first step on any journey.

Unintentional creation, the idea that fate is dictated by a person's natural disposition, well I call BS. We all steer our own boat. No matter your natural disposition or life experience, you can influence how you feel through intentional choices and daily habits that raise your vibration and position you to receive the very gifts you most easily give.

It's easy to think that the Rich's of the world are lucky, but they too have weak links. Because events generally work out in their favor – even though they be might watered-down versions of what they actually desire - they can get a little lazy with manifestation as they rely solely on the good nature of the personality they were born with. And as we know, the human part of life can be stressful. Without intentional high vibration habits in place, stress will chisel away at that good nature.

And so, you might think that the opposite end of the spectrum is the unlucky one, because they have to be more intentional with high vibration habits. However, folks that have more to lose are much more inspired and motivated to rise above and stay the course. Their desire for a better way is so strong, it puts them in a position to connect to joy profoundly.

"Imagine within each of us there lies two beasts," says a wise grandmother to her grandchild.

"A positive beast that lifts us up and connects us to opportunities, helpers, kindness, laughter, and love, and a negative beast that breaks us down and connects us to anger, resentment, and jealousy."

The child asks which beast will win.

The grandmother replies: "Whichever beast you feed."

Through using a formula for achieving physical, mental, emotional and spiritual balance, we have centered our work in the realm of **intentional creation,** which is choosing to get a few steps in front of life and feed the positive beast within.

As you strengthen your sense of self, you make intentional choices to make you feel good knowing the positive effects they pull forth. A very powerful position indeed! However, this is just the tip of the manifesting iceberg.

Weeding through what we don't want, in order to discover what we truly want, is a necessary and powerful step, as opposites define one another.

However, intentional creation can get lodged in transactional and conditional outcomes. Here are some examples:

- You desire to be healthy, but your intention of exercising is to look good.

- You desire to feel God's presence, but your intention of meditating is to destress.
- You desire to feel abundant, but your intention of manifesting is to get $1million.
- You desire to feel nourished, but your intention of eating healthy is to lose weight.

What's wrong with these intentions? They don't match. Looking good does not manifest health. Resilience to stress does not connect you to God. One million dollars will not solely make you feel abundant and losing weight will not make you feel whole. As it becomes harder and harder to manifest your desires in this way, you will experience frustration, impatience, and question what's the point of all this sacrifice.

Your intention for choosing to do anything should be simply because it makes you feel better than you did before.

Deliberate creation

- You desire to feel healthy, so you choose to exercise because it makes you feel healthy. When you feel healthy, you are healthy.
- You desire to feel God's presence, so you choose to quiet your mind in meditation and connect to God. You feel at peace therefore you are at peace.
- You desire to feel abundant, so you choose to open yourself to the surrounding abundance. You feel abundant, so you are abundant.
- You desire to feel nourished, so you choose to eat food that makes you feel satiated. You feel satisfied, so you are satisfied.

Here, we change our way of being and achieve health, peace, and abundance without force. The positive beast has already won, this is your new nature.

Consider that the universe is already in alignment, and God is always present. All you have to do is connect to this life force.

The following chapters outline a few key ways to work through and shine light on your blind spots.

CHAPTER 24

Unleash False Beliefs

"Watch your thoughts, they become words. Watch your words, they become action. Watch your actions, they become habits. Watch your habits, they become character. Watch your character, it becomes your destiny."
—Lao Tzu

My older sister, Laura is an exceptional and successful artist. I swear she was born an artist. Nine years my senior, she fascinated me as a kid with her non-stop creating and swirl of friends always around. Don't tell her, but I secretly wanted to be a cool artist just like her.

Somewhere along the way I pegged "cool artists" as wild, nonchalant, laid back, and spontaneous and in my haste to this aspiration I picked up some bad habits. I was disorganized, spacey, too laid back, too wild, notoriously late, and the kind of person who over promised and under delivered.

It was a lot of fun.

(I know she's going to read this, so I just want to clarify that Laura did not model these problematic behaviors – I nurtured them all on my own!)

I was also hanging on to some false beliefs, namely: Being cool meant not giving a shit and artists have special permission to be hot messes.

In design school, I strung together semester-long assignments at the last possible moment. I missed classes and was often caught by surprise by exams that were clearly communicated by my teachers. On one occasion a teacher went so far as to pull me aside to say, "it's time to clean up your act."

I scoffed. This is who I am! A person who drives around with the gas light on, too busy and too careless to make investments in my own self.

I ran on fumes and always coming up from behind. It was my way, and it defined my personality. I made light of my bad behavior with friends and family. It was cool, because I was cool. Except for those times when I ran out of excuses and gas. Then all I felt was inadequate and a failure.

Of course, I was jealous of my peers who received praise and attention for their accomplishments and dedication to work. I would tell myself I didn't care, as I saw their sacrifice, but deep down, I wished I had what it took to put true effort into my work.

Deep down I believed in my talent, but I was so accustomed to getting by that breaking the cycle seemed impossible. It's also what others came to expect from me, which made the cycle even harder to break.

Age and yoga helped curve this reactionary living a little, as a lot of tough lessons forced me to evaluate the difference between nurtured habits vs my actual nature. *I am the creator of my experience*; set in and I made some pivotal changes. Like becoming a morning person, for one.

Early in my teaching I stepped up to teach the 6AM class. My sisters and old friends were shocked, and I was too, for that matter, because that meant waking up 4:30AM to get there on time. But after about a month, my body adjusted, and I felt clear and energized like never before. I was supposed to be a night owl! A light bulb went off and I thought to myself, what else can I train my body and mind to do? And that set me off on a series of small but pivotal adjustments that made me feel empowered, accomplished, resilient, inspired, and joyful!

Looking back, I realize how this false belief I attached to as a little kid never felt right because it denied me my core values. Freedom, for one, because my choices were limited due to lack of effort. Authenticity because I wasn't living up to my talents and gifts, and abundance is obvious. I paid little attention to my health, and honestly, if I had honored that one part, the rest would have self-corrected. No one told me about how my emotions are an indicator if I'm aligned with my inner-being, my true nature.

So, you can see how this one tiny false belief manifested a plethora of commotion.

What false beliefs have you shed along the way? Are you holding any still?

A few common ones that come up frequently in my work are; I'm not enough, perfection being tied to worthiness, life is hard, and you can't trust anyone.

It's definitely beneficial to recognize them but go a little deeper and see if you can get specific as to how it impacts you as this forges a clearer path to truth.

Practicum

Spend your quiet time today, or over the next few days — as long as it takes — to contemplate a belief that has held you back from meeting your desires. Work backward to get to the root.

What habits hold you back? When did those habits creep up? Connect habits to an idea, a person, a thought, an experience. Get to the bottom to pull up the root!

Journal or just think about the ways in which you hedge your own success. As you do this, please be aware and take care not to shame yourself. Shame can costume itself as awareness, but shame robs us of inspiration and worth.

Shame is a trickster. Nevertheless, pay close attention as you spend time with the parts of your story that bring up difficult feelings. You certainly don't need to be afraid of owning your false beliefs, take care with yourself and applaud yourself for your honesty.

Write your false belief and truth below. I left space for a few.

I hold the false belief that

_____

_____

My new belief is

_____

_____

I hold the false belief that

_____

_____

My new belief is

_____

_____

I hold the false belief that

_____

_____

My new belief is

_____

_____

Embody your new beliefs. Play with them in meditation. Try repeating some affirmations like "The belief that I am not enough is false. The truth is, I am enough."

Play with the wording until it's accurate and your own. Keep it simple and repeat the truth throughout your day, whenever a false belief creeps into your mind, habits or way of being.

Remember your formula for grounding yourself with physical, mental, emotional and spiritual exercises to continue to drive your new belief home. Be aware of how false beliefs impede you from your commitments to your well-being.

CHAPTER 25

Unleash A-Little-Bit-A-Lot

"Your net worth to the world is usually determined
by what remains after your bad habits are
subtracted from your good habits."
—Benjamin Franklin

On one hand I was experiencing success as a yoga teacher, but on the other hand, that breakthrough came with shame, like I had really screwed up by wasting so much time with my false beliefs. I was embarrassed by my historical lack of discipline and believed I should be punished for my poor choices.

So, I threw achievement at everything. I set goals and took challenges head on, I made hard work the big thing about me. I had the bull by the horns.

But you can't actually hold on to a bull for very long. Burn out was shredding me, and my first clue that I still had some blind spots.

Burn out is a clue that too much attention is focused on strengthening your weakest link.

In martial arts, a weak link is made strong through repetition, over short periods of time. But a novice like myself will always first try to force a way to perfection. Dripping in sweat, frustrated, and exhausted, and still trying like hell to execute a deflecting strike, Roger stood calmly by, repeating only two words over and over: Effortless effort.

Roger could be super annoying like that. How the hell could I exert all my strength and energy effortlessly? Intellectually, however, I did understand what he meant, despite the fact I could not feel it in my body.

Until, inevitably, the breakthrough did come. "I did it! How did I do that? How do I do it again?" And just like that, I was back to trying, figuring it out, forcing, and muscling through. Roger would say again patiently... effortless effort.

Later in my journey another teacher said, "A-little-bit-a-lot goes a long way." And I immediately thought of Roger and his patient steady guidance as he modeled what a lifelong practice looks like.

"Focus on one thing at a time, fine tune a little every day, and simply enjoy the process," he would say.

The gap between muscling and fluidity will get shorter and shorter with time as long as you trust the process – A-little-bit-a-lot.

Reflection practicum

Take a pause to recall your desires. Reflect on the weak links in your daily habits that keep you from actualizing your desires. Remember how false beliefs can create weak habits.

How can the mantra, a-little-bit-a-lot, help you break down an overwhelming goal into simple, short, doable tasks?

Allow the mantra, a-little-bit-a-lot, to slow you down. Take time to remind yourself of your success thus far. We started with building exercise, meditation, and nourishment practice for a reason: Tangible activities foster a clear mind and well-being.

Nature + Nurture

Expansion is achieved when we honor both our natural gifts while also paying mind to our weak spots with daily habits.

Think of it as making a major shift in your trajectory, one degree at a time.

When I finally accepted that we're on this earth to create, that early lesson Roger taught me, how well-being is both science and art, finally landed. I thought to myself, "Wait, I can create whatever I want? I can be whatever I want? I can go about it in my unique way? In fact, if I do it my way it will be much easier and fulfilling! It is my work of art!"

You see, this whole time I was shaming and punishing myself for not being disciplined enough. Successful people have discipline and I wanted to be successful, so I read articles, countless books, and paid close attention to how my successful friends operated in life. I picked up some good advice, but in my head, they were enough, and I wasn't and along the way I dampened one of my strongest qualities… my ability to be carefree. But truly, lack of discipline was holding me back, so I couldn't just shirk it because it wasn't natural to me.

After some contemplating, I realized that the word discipline feels rigid to me – not good - so I had to reword it. My husband is a highly disciplined person and one day he said, "It's just a choice I make." And that right there hit the nail on the head. He doesn't resist what needs to be done in order to accomplish what's important to him. He just does it and consistently, so it's not a big deal. The idea of discipline being a choice felt freeing – a core value of mine.

Here in lies effortless effort.

So, a-little-bit-a-lot, with my trajectory set, I made the choice to take small but pivotal steps *my way*. I certainly bump up against my old ways of procrastinating from time to time but resolve to get back on track as soon as I notice I'm off course - not the next work day or following Monday - as soon as the awareness hits me.

Reflection

Spend time reminding yourself of your natural talents and gifts. Celebrate the details of your personality that *you* love — not necessarily what other people love about you!

I love that I...

The qualities I love most about myself...

Manifestation Practicum

Are you a procrastinator or a grinder? Find flow and ease with this technique...

Get out a few sheets of paper and pick a few life categories you're working on - career, friendships, hobbies, finances – and give a whole sheet for each category. Then, write tasks associated with that particular category that you could complete that week – in no particular order or importance.

When you feel resistance, go to your sheet(s) and pick one task that you really want to do, sounds fun, easy and/or enjoyable - pick the task with the least resistance.

The magic of this is that it raises your vibration and your work is quality. Feeling good and quality work – the ultimate space for expansion!

CHAPTER 26

Unleash Expansion

*"Ever since I was a child I have had this instinctive
urge for experience and growth. To me the function
and duty of a quality human being is the sincere
and honest development of one's potential."*
—Bruce Lee

I will never finish creating or expanding my world.

And go ahead and throw all the cliches on the table. I love them all!

Life is a journey not a destination; Life is a marathon; Life is a song — we each get to write our own lyrics; Life is a puzzle — you can only see the picture when you put all the pieces together. Life is a garden — with care and love you can cultivate beautiful flowers.

Not gonna lie though. The idea of never being done did exhaust me at first.

The satisfaction of completing something is deeply ingrained in our psyche. From schooling to graduating to marrying, to birthing, to retiring — society teaches us that these are all chapters to be completed. Pages to turn.

But imagine instead the expansion of never stopping. Imagine the joy in endless learning, exploring, curiosity, understanding, strengthening, loving, empathizing, creating. Exhaustion is rooted in fear. If you believe that life is hard, then yes, an endless slog of suffering it may very well be.

But don't get me wrong, I agree it can be hard being human. But then there's laughter, experience, beauty, love, exploration, and joy — the nature of our beings, the gift of our beautiful planet!

A-little-bit-a-lot. Take, small but meaningful steps to revel in your life every day. Honor your values. Adjust as needed. Every moment offers an opportunity to learn more about your body, mind, emotions, and spirit, and the people you share your world with. Use the formula you've built to help establish and maintain nourishing habits.

Last Thoughts... **The path of least resistance**

Let's say you hate exercise.

You desire to be physically healthy, but you hate exercise. You do it begrudgingly. You do it because you're supposed to. The vibration you bring to exercise does not match the vibration of good health, therefore, you miss out on the experience of physical health through exercise.

Over time you warm up to exercise, but only a little. You appreciate how you feel afterward, so you do it, but with some resistance. Your vibration has improved, but still not a winning match.

Apply that scenario to other activities.

The desire for financial freedom, while also holding a block against learning about money management.

The desire to fall in love, only you don't even enjoy your own company.

The desire to experience less stress, but with a cynicism for meditation.

A desire to eat healthier, without the will to cook.

A clean house, without a commitment to organize.

This manual is designed to close the gap between values and desires. I believe it's the gap between our values and desires that stifles so many people. I know it to have been true for me.

I hope by now you have come to see that discipline is just another word for choice. My greatest wish for you is that you find your path of least resistance and enjoy everywhere it takes you.

Bliss is your birthright.

Bliss is fulfillment.

Fulfilled individuals change the world.

Ask. Nurture. Evolve. Expand. Fulfillment. Repeat.

We're all on this together.

And I truly mean together! Join our community at JaymeYoga.com

Printed in the United States
by Baker & Taylor Publisher Services